THE WAY *of the* WARRIOR Mama

Praises for *The Way of the Warrior Mama*

"There is a generation of passionate #metoo mamas, trying to sort out how to raise sexually healthy, happy, empowered girls.
In *The Way of the Warrior Mama*, Sally Clark brings a first-hand account to this dilemma with compassion and integrity."

—**Sharon Maxwell**, Ph.D. author of *The Talk: A Breakthrough Guide to Raising Kids in on Over-Sexualized, Online, In-Your-Face World*

"Sally walks the delicate line between every parents anxiety of sexual violence being directed towards their daughter and balances this with giving hope and practical advice. Most of all this book can serve as a calming and clear guide to help you know the right thing to say as your girl grows into young womanhood. As a father of two daughters I am grateful for the ground that this book breaks."

—**Kim John Payne**, M.ED, author of *Simplicity Parenting* and *The Soul of Discipline*

THE WAY *of the*
WARRIOR
Mama

The Guide to
Protecting and Raising
STRONG DAUGHTERS

SALLY CLARK

NEW YORK

LONDON • NASHVILLE • MELBOURNE • VANCOUVER

THE WAY *of the* WARRIOR Mama
The Guide to Protecting and Raising STRONG DAUGHTERS©
2019 SALLY CLARK

Published in New York, New York, by Morgan James Publishing in partnership with Difference Press. Morgan James is a trademark of Morgan James, LLC. www.MorganJamesPublishing.com

The Morgan James Speakers Group can bring authors to your live event. For more information or to book an event visit The Morgan James Speakers Group at www.TheMorganJamesSpeakersGroup.com.

ISBN 978-1-68350-997-4 paperback
ISBN 978-1-68350-998-1 eBook
Library of Congress Control Number: 2018934773

Cover Design by:
Rachel Lopez
www.r2cdesign.com

Interior Design by:
Bonnie Bushman
The Whole Caboodle Graphic Design

In an effort to support local communities, raise awareness and funds, Morgan James Publishing donates a percentage of all book sales for the life of each book to Habitat for Humanity Peninsula and Greater Williamsburg.

Get involved today! Visit
www.MorganJamesBuilds.com

To my daughters, Giada and Sienna.

TABLE OF CONTENTS

INTRODUCTION

The front of our old refrigerator looks like a typical cluttered fridge in a busy household with children. There are children's drawings pinned up: a Chinese New Year's celebration frame with my daughter as a four-year-old in preschool, a photo of my two girls with their grandma, a magnet chore chart that hasn't been used in at least a year, an old grocery list, and random souvenir magnets from various family vacations. It's a bit of a mess, but all in all, if the fridge is sending any message about our family it's that life isn't too bad. We're holding it together and we're managing to have some fun in the process.

But there, mixed in the clutter, is a faded, almost grey magnet of a naked woman—the naked goddess Aphrodite. I bought Aphrodite in the heyday of my thirty-something single years living in New York City, finally coming into my own as a woman, coming into my career, dating, taking self-improvement classes of all kinds, learning about goddesses, and enjoying the single life. Back then, Aphrodite was skin-colored and standing on top of a clam shell. She came with different clothes, like a paper doll, but part of the fun was undressing her and showing her beautiful, nude body on my fridge.

Thirteen years later, Aphrodite is still here, but her skin color has paled to the point where she looks ill or corpse-like and her clothes have long since disappeared to the island of lost toys and other doodads. Little fingers have bent her body to the point where one day, Aphrodite lost her feet. She's not looking her best these days, but I am determined to keep her on that damn fridge! Is it age, or is it the constant worrying about her daughters that has caused Aphrodite to turn grey? Have her efforts to chase after her daughters and raise them well caused her to lose her own footing, her own ground? Her devotion to them is clear: she will sacrifice her clothes, expose herself to the world, and do anything to protect her little goddesses once they turn into women, but it seems her devotion has turned to desperation.

Maybe you couldn't care less about Aphrodite but you can relate to the incessant worrying about your daughters becoming teenagers and then experiencing sexual trauma. This book offers a roadmap to help you navigate the rocky terrain of parenting an adolescent girl. In no way do I mean to diminish the importance or the challenges of raising an adolescent boy. Sexual assault and the rape of boys and men remain a serious problem in our society. It is my wish that this book will help you have faith that you and your daughter can survive the teenage years.

At the beginning of this, you will realize that you are not alone in experiencing extreme anxiety in parenting a teen in light of the alarming rate of date rape and sexual abuse among teens in this country. You will learn about my journey and the relationship between my own healing and protecting my daughters. You do have cause to be frightened, but you will see that there are hacks moms use to help them keep calm and carry on. You will learn how to turn what might be your worst enemy—your mind—into your best ally.

Further along, you will learn about the protective power of sisterhood. In Chapter 6, I'll outline ways to treat your own body like a sacred temple. In Chapter 7, you will learn about all things goddess-related and how this can you help you and your daughter. In Chapter 8, I will outline common obstacles in the odyssey of protecting your daughter and becoming fearless. Finally, in Chapter 9: Unleash the Tigress, you will see how to lead a juicy, sexy life while at the same time serving as a role model for your daughter.

Among parents comparing the difference between raising a boy versus a girl, you hear sayings like, "With a boy you pay early, but with a girl you pay later [once she reaches adolescence]." I remember that when my daughter was a toddler, I was talking with another mom about moms getting back to a more normal life once their baby was a little older, and a mom of a boy saying, "The moms with girls start wearing makeup sooner." I also remember seeing moms of toddler boys looking even more haggard than us pretty tired-looking moms of toddler girls. I felt sorry for them and then silently breathed a sigh of relief. I found myself laughing and joking with other people who talked about how wonderful it was to have little girls, but "just wait until they're teenagers!" they'd say with a look of half-serious frustration and mock horror. As my girls got a little older, my joking and smiling started to be a little more forced. It wasn't quite so funny once the realization that my girls becoming teens was right around the corner.

Chapter 1

THEY'RE COMING FOR HER ON HORSEBACK

The phenomenon is so shocking that later, years after I read about it, I started to think it was a hoax.

In Kazakhstan, it is still common practice for a man to kidnap a woman to be his bride, despite it being outlawed in 1994. The kidnapping used to be done on horseback, but now is mostly done by car. Many of these abductions are violent, with the kidnappers forcing the woman to go to his family's house to meet her groom-to-be's family, and for hours she is psychologically pressured to submit to marriage. Often just the fact that she has been taken to the groom's house puts her honor and virginity in question so that even if she leaves, her reputation is tarnished. Most women relent, and few kidnappings are ever prosecuted.

I'm still waiting for someone to announce that this nightmarish Kazakhstani reality is all a farce, like something you would see in that satirical comedy *Borat* about a Kazakh journalist played by British comedian Sacha Cohen. If only we could all wake up one day to discover that it was a sick, surreal joke and, after a sigh of relief and maybe a little chuckle, we could go back to our Western, living-inside-a-developed-country, bubble lives.

As I thought more carefully about bride kidnapping, it made me wonder what the lives of these little Kazakhstani girls are like. These girls must begin to get nervous as they approach the age of 16 and the end of high school. But when they are little, is life pretty carefree? How do their mothers feel? While they raise their daughters from infancy to age 12 or so, do they remain in denial about the fact that one day their own daughters may be traumatized just as they once were?

Our culture has made great strides in educating parents on how to raise strong, confident girls, from sending the message of "girl power" during the 1990s to dispelling the myths and stereotypes of girls in the recent "#Like a Girl" campaign. From girls' leadership programs to female super hero characters like Wonder Woman and underdogs turned heroines like Katniss Everdeen, role models and paths to female leadership do exist. Similarly, with Title IV promoting equality in girls' sports and the continuing effort to motivate girls to study STEM and other initiatives to level the playing field for girls, we moms can feel somewhat equipped and supported in our quest to raise super-girls—at least, until our daughters hit puberty. While by no means an easy endeavor, on most days we feel like, *hey I got this*.

Then we read about another date rape scandal on a college campus or hear about what happened at a recent unchaperoned high school party. A presidential candidate recorded on tape joking about grabbing a women's private parts is elected the leader of this country and put in charge of tending the great garden where all our budding super-girl flowers are expected to grow and blossom. It starts to feel like all of this girl power, "girl you can do anything" training is all for naught as we send our daughter off to her first big co-ed party or send her off to college. Are we sending her off to the slaughter? Are we deceiving our little girls?

For any parent, there is nothing more devastating than seeing one's child suffer. In moments of darkness and despair, in an attempt to spare our daughters from experiencing the soul-crushing experience of having one's wings clipped or, worse, ripped from them, we may ignore the protests of the ardent feminists within us. For a brief moment of delusion, we may contemplate "drinking the Kool-Aid" by sheltering our daughters and teaching them from an early age that they are dependent, meek, and inferior. We may question whether or not to teach our little girls to fly at all. As in a horror or sci-fi movie or nightmare, this distorted vision of protecting our girls can seem for a moment like an idyllic fairy tale scene, with little girls donning pretty perfectly hemmed dresses and singing and running outside in a meadow with birds chirping on a picture-perfect, sunny summer day. Yet something is off in this scene.

Maybe the girls are singing too perfectly in an almost robotic fashion. Maybe the birds that seemed so colorful and bright are slightly sinister. Maybe there is a dark cloud appearing in the distance. Maybe the sun has been shining too long. Then we awake from the nightmare. We realize that harboring this delusion is to *protect us* from experiencing the pain of seeing our children suffer.

You may, like me, feel an underlying ache gnawing inside of you not unlike the way a Kazakhstani mother might feel as her daughter takes one step closer to hitting puberty. In case anyone, including your inner critic, tells you to stop agonizing because the situation is not *that* dire, here are some disturbing statistics: one in five women will be raped at some point in their lives. Nearly one in three teenage girls reports having survived sexual violence. Females aged 16-19 are four times more likely than the general population to be victims of rape. Despite the many gains in the women's movement, sexual violence is still a very real chilling part of our culture's underbelly.

I won't inundate you with more statistics—some of which you have probably already read or heard about—but it is worth remembering that behind the numbers are real girls and women. It is depressing and even morbid to go there, but translating these cold statistics into more human terms shows the greater urgency with which we need to protect our girls. In other words, five out of the 25 little elementary school girls at the next birthday party you attend are likely to be sexually assaulted at some point in their lifetime. Given that rape and sexual assault are notoriously underreported (36 percent of rapes, 34 percent of attempted rapes, and only 26 percent of sexual assaults are reported), we can safely assume that the numbers are much higher. We spend so much of our time worrying about our children's and our own health, and yet a woman is twice as more likely to be raped than she is to develop breast cancer.

I, like most people, am grateful for technology and the Internet and recognize that they are powerful tools that can be used to better the world, however, when I think of parenting an adolescent, I admit that I am almost resentful at this new, complicated entity that has made educating teens about sex and keeping teens safe exponentially harder. Ask any expert on child and adolescent development what they think are the biggest obstacles today's parents face, and they will tell you that those obstacles are the media and our consumerist culture. Now that the Internet, cell phones, and social media reign supreme in the lives of every teen, sexual predators, sexual harassers, and bullies are like viruses or parasites that have a found whole new ecology in which to find new ways to survive, to replicate themselves, or to hide or find new hosts to live in.

Not only do we parents have to protect our kids from online sexual predators, we now also have to worry about our children being bullied and/or sexually harassed online by their peers. One out of every four girls has been sent unwelcome sexual comments, pictures, and jokes, or had someone post something inappropriate about them online. One of the most common forms of sexual harassment among middle and high schoolers is "slut shaming," stigmatizing a girl or woman for sexually provocative behavior or behavior deemed as promiscuous. Without ever being physically touched, countless girls and women can be emotionally scarred for life by being called a slut in person or, even more sinisterly, by the simple click of a sent text.

Add physical and sexual violence and there is further cause for angst. The long-term effects of date rape and other trauma that can alter a young woman's life forever. Survivors are four times more likely to abuse drugs, three times more likely to experience a major depressive episode as adults, and four times more likely to develop PTSD (Post Traumatic Stress Disorder) symptoms, the same symptoms often suffered by military veterans after battle. How do we arm our girls for this kind of battle?

When they are children, we feed them fairytales, fables, and princess stories, none of which ever feature a Cinderella or a Snow White learning how to defend themselves against sexual predators or suffering from the aftermath of trauma. There is no fairy godmother to magically cure the after-effects of sexual trauma: extreme guilt, depression, shame, eating disorders, sleep disorders, anxiety, dissociative patterns where they feel disconnected from reality and from their bodies, repression, denial, sexual problems, and relationship problems. Depression remains the most common long-term problem among survivors. Given the fact that it is still not culturally acceptable for a woman to express her anger without being called a "bitch" or even assert herself without being labeled "aggressive" in the business world and elsewhere, even women who haven't experienced trauma get depressed. But subject them to trauma, and the depth of depression can implode inside them.

Why and how survivors exhibit different symptoms is worthy of another book, but the pink elephant in the room that has to be a major cause of sexual trauma survivors internalizing their devastation is the fact that even *if* they have the courage to report their rape, there is a belief that very few rapists will go to jail. Many survivors don't report rape because they don't believe it will make any difference, and given society's tendency to place the blame on the victim, why would they want to risk being further traumatized?

Whether you are raising teenage boys or teenage girls, it is known and practically accepted as a given in our culture that parenting a teen is extremely stressful. Just hearing about the various stresses of parenting teens from my older siblings—spending many sleepless nights lying awake worrying about their teenage sons and daughters being out at a party, for example—scared me off from having kids. Then, when preparing for my own marriage, I learned about how marital happiness plummets when children become teens. I conveniently repressed that factoid since I found having and raising babies and toddlers challenging enough.

Each generation of girls and boys face unique challenges to their time. The Baby Boomers faced the threat of nuclear war and the burgeoning of civil rights. Generation X confronted the AIDS epidemic and the tearing down of the Berlin Wall. The Millennial generation was transformed overnight by 9/11 and an instant gratification mindset. Today's Generation Z faces climate change and life after the Great Recession. Nevertheless, other challenges endure, just masked in slightly different forms. One of these is the pressure on girls to be "the good girl": selfless, popular, successful but polite (too polite, as Rachel Simmons's *The Curse of the Good Girl* shows, this pressure to conform to a narrow ideal of femininity is terrifying when seen how it plays out in sexual assault). During the 2016 trial of a New Hampshire senior student who was accused of raping a then-15-year-old freshman, the survivor explained that she had tried to say no "as politely as possible" at least three times. She was polite because she didn't want to appear "rude or "bitchy."

Fairytales continue to be popular, and while there is some backlash—Peggy Orenstein's *Cinderella Ate My Daughter* being an example—the princess culture continues to grow. Girls are still taught they are made of "sugar and spice and everything nice," and that most princesses have Barbie doll anatomies and get rescued by the prince. To some extent, girls have been taught they can be strong and that they can do anything they want to if they set their minds to it, yet they still receive the message that they must also somehow be nice and good at the same time. The rite of passage from girlhood to womanhood is now even more complicated.

Chapter 2

MY STORY

A breakthrough moment for me happened inside a Red Tent at a women's festival I attended with my good friends and our daughters. The Red Tent movement originated from the Moon Lodge or Menstrual Hut, a concept that dates back to 800 C.E. when women in tribal cultures would gather during menstruation, often considered a sacred time, and sometimes call upon their ancestors and/or higher powers to ask for guidance. Today, Red Tents are offered around the world and open to women during any time of their cycle to retreat from the masculine, unending "doing" mindset and just be. Women may relax, talk, sleep, sip tea, dance, meditate, and often open up to each other or themselves in a safe, nurturing way. There is something enchanting about a group of women gathering together.

In this one, the atmosphere was like that of a typical Red Tent: sensual, soothing, intoxicating, and thoroughly womb-like in the way it made me feel safe and protected. It was a nighttime, post-festival celebration, and our little girls were dancing around in the little nooks and crannies of the red space. Our girls were drawn to the Red Tent like fireflies to the light, they kept wanting to return there. Their pure, unadulterated, non-rationalizing minds openly soaked in the palpable, positive feminine energy. I had been in the Red Tent earlier the same day, attending a workshop where a group of women had shared their various stories of heart wrenching pain—everything from being disowned by their parents for having a baby out of wedlock to rape.

After absorbing all of the pain, the laughter, and the intense, penultimate commiserating over and ultimately celebrating of what it means to be a woman in the Western world, the experience finally made a dent in the armor I thought I'd shed a long time ago. I lay on one of the soft, velvety couches and broke down sobbing. All the emotion was too much for my psyche, my spirit, and my body to take. My good friends caught wind of my emotional crumbling and deftly shuffled my girls away to another corner of the room, giving me the space to fall to pieces. I just lost it. I told myself it was just the wine I'd had while celebrating in our cabin to get dressed up for the festival party. But my deeper self knew. Of course I was experiencing the stress most mothers must experience from carrying the weight and responsibility of having to care for her children, but there was a deeper level of anxiety that surfaced. I realized right then and there that I was utterly terrified about my daughters becoming teenagers and being sexually assaulted. Just the idea of anyone laying a hand on my baby girls was almost excruciatingly painful. I also realized that if I was feeling this way now, there was no way I was going to be able to hold it together once my girls actually reached their teen years.

Why was the idea of this so excruciating? Because at the age of 15, I was date raped. A freshman at a co-ed boarding school and an athletic, artistic honors student who some teachers called "sunny," "vivacious," and "well-rounded," I had spent my first year away at boarding school making friends, including a couple of different boyfriends—all pretty innocent. By the end of the school year I had fallen in love and had a serious boyfriend.

Then summer came. One night, my friend invited me up to her cabin. I lied and told my mom that my friend's parents would be there. Thrilled to have gotten away with our ruse, we went up to the cabin. Two boys—one of them from our junior high days—heard we were partying up at the cabin without our parents, so they came up. We smoked pot. We started drinking early in the afternoon. The last I remembered, I was holding a glass of wine and listening to this boy talk about his ex-girlfriend. Then I blacked out. I remember nothing from the rest of that evening.

I woke up in bed very hung over and confused. My clothes were on, but something was off. The other boy had been upstairs with my girlfriend. Once everyone woke up, it was clear something was awry by the way both boys—well, really the one boy—bolted out of that cabin as if fleeing the scene of a crime. He *was* fleeing the scene of the crime. He knew what he did. I was still stunned, partly by the hangover. But I think the trauma or shock in my mind and body was so intense that I was numb. Everything seemed fine until I took a shower, and then I knew what had happened. A deep, sickening wave of blackness and sheer dread welled up inside of me as I realized I had been raped.

Without consciously being aware of it, I made a decision to bury this pain so deeply that I was in denial of it happening for years. I categorically denied it. It did *not happen.* Years later, when I was finally able to utter the word "rape," I asked my therapist how I could have repressed it and just carried on like nothing happened. It was like I was mad at myself for not suffering or showing my pain more. I remember her explaining that this kind of trauma is too much for an adolescent to process. Suppression is a kind of survival and coping mechanism.

Only weeks before the incident, I had been worried about my friends' well-being and cautioning them to be careful and use birth control, as they were starting to have sex with their boyfriends. Now the sunny, well-rounded girl had a deep dark cloud that she kept hidden. Perhaps the one thing that gave it away was the contrast between my freshman school picture— where I was almost giggling as I posed for the portrait with an asymmetrical new wave haircut and my eyes sparkling with joy—and my sophomore portrait, in which I had a nice, clean 1980s bob and was wearing the British-influenced boarding school blazer uniform. A nice, responsible, attractive young woman, but the light in my eyes had dulled. I never told anyone what had happened until 15 years later, at the age of 30.

For years, I dated verbally abusive and controlling men. My feminist awakenings and the stirring anger started to surface during my college junior year abroad in France and while traveling Europe, especially in southern countries like Italy and Greece where men take cat calls to a wholly different, disturbing level in the form of hissing. Even up north on a Paris subway, a North American demeanor with a smile is interpreted as an open invitation to be harassed. Ironically, it was in France that I came into my sexuality, but also into my feminism. On the one hand, men were more openly chauvinistic, yet on the other hand, the culture on the whole was more open about sexuality. There wasn't the puritanical strain of not talking as openly about sex, of covering up one's bodily odors, etc. So while I started to blossom in my sexuality and gain confidence from living in a foreign country, underneath I was still angry and very insecure. I was involved in a turbulent relationship with a Frenchman that last several years. It was during our heart-wrenching and almost devastating break-up, when I moved to New York for graduate school, that I started to realize how much I had internalized my rape and blamed myself for it. Despite counselling and therapy, it was only when I went to a retreat at the Esalen Institute and sat inside a yurt for a Gestalt session (pretty normal thing to do while in the context of Esalen) that I became aware of how much I judged the 15-year-old girl I was when I was date raped.

Like many single New Yorkers, I enjoyed living the liberating life of a single woman working in New York. I had great girlfriends and guy friends. I was doing therapy and taking a number of different self-help courses and workshops. Thanks to the many different courses and therapies I tried, I became better at judging what it was to be treated respectfully in a relationship. I had a much better idea of what a healthy love relationship really was. I became involved in another serious relationship with the man who would become my husband. While we shared an openness from having taken the same self-improvement leadership course (at different times), he could sense that I still felt unresolved with and distant from my parents. There was something holding me back from fully feeling like I could be myself with them and be open with them. It took me orchestrating a family therapy session for me to finally open up to them about what had happened. From then on, it was like a weight had been lifted, and I felt freer with my parents and siblings. I think it took that for my boyfriend to see that I was ready to heal. He then proposed shortly afterwards.

I had indeed healed a great deal, but when I became pregnant with my first child there was a very clear signal deep inside of me that I had a whole hell of a lot more healing to do. I would pray that I would give birth to a boy. I couldn't admit to anyone, not even my husband, that I didn't want have a girl because I couldn't handle the pain that she would endure from being born a female. I knew how hard it would be for her. I never realized until about six or seven years later, at the women's festival where I had the Red Tent epiphany, that I clearly needed to face the fact that I had deeper healing to do.

It was at my breakdown in the Red Tent that an angel named Meg Tobin said, "Here's my number. Contact me, we can work through your anxiety." Despite my tears just a moment earlier, I was still for some reason surprised that she thought I was anxious. But I contacted her and told my husband I was taking a week off away from him and my girls. I worked with Meg and started unraveling the fact that underneath, I was still brimming with anxiety. I did not feel safe in my body.

Chapter 3
THE PATH TO PROTECTION

Y ou do not need have to have experienced rape or sexual trauma to feel scared and anxious about how to protect your teenage daughter. You and I know all too well that my story and that of countless other females (and males) is far too common. Where is the middle ground between burying our heads in the sand and hoping our daughters emerge from adolescence relatively unscathed (which, sadly, means still probably experiencing an unwanted, demeaning touch, remark, or cat call in the street by virtue of being female), and being in a perpetual state of panic and policing our girls, forever anticipating the worst and sheltering them from every possible danger? The question remains: how do we protect our daughters? After speaking with experts, wise older crone mamas, and younger mamas—some trauma survivors, some not—and learning from my own healing journey, I've created a general roadmap with major landmarks to guide you and help keep you and your daughter on track.

Our desire to protect our young starts in utero. Even before our child is born, we parents are in protection mode, worrying about how to keep the unborn fetus safe from all the various evils, including unhealthy diet, BPA products, raw seafood, etc. While there are many different parenting philosophies rest assured that if you want some guidance, you can find a book to help you. You can find many books on how to parent an adolescent, too. What parenting experts, therapists, experienced mothers, and women survivors all emphasize is teaching your children boundaries and using their voice. Girls need to know that their voices will be heard early on, long before the teenage years. As therapist, trauma resiliency expert, and mother of four Meg Tobin explains, you can start helping your teenage daughter at as young as age two:

> *"You start to give them a foundation where they feel like they have agency in their own lives. Where they feel like when they say, 'No,' it's respected. When they feel like when they open their mouths what they say matters. All of those things are laying a foundation for them to say, 'Get away from me. I don't want you touching my body.' As opposed to a kid who's going to be frozen. Like, 'I don't ever have*

*an experience of saying no and being respected or heard so
I don't know what to do.'"*

Almost every day, kids are figuring out their boundaries and learning that they have a *choice.* Gestalt psychotherapist Alison Stone, mother of two daughters, shares her wisdom:

*"Where I live, they started in preschool. If a child
grabbed another child by the arm and said, 'Come over
here,' they would say, 'But Jennifer makes decisions about
Jennifer's body.'"*

Learning to Say No to an Unsolicited Hug

We spend an inordinate amount of time teaching girls to be nice and respect others, and not enough time on how to respect themselves, their bodies, and their minds. If all we tell our girls is that they are made of sugar and spice and everything nice and that in life you have to smile, say yes, and be agreeable, then we are training them to be victims. Sometimes the answer lies in the ability to say yes or no to a hug. In writer, storyteller, and teacher Jamie Waggoner's Artemis's workshop, girls learn about:

*"A goddess who is very empowered in her maidenhood,
in her girlhood, womanhood, she's all about boundaries,
working with nature and putting your sights on what
you want. Those are kind of her big three lessons and
unapologetically going for what you want. Those are some
pretty good lessons for girls, right?"*

Jamie tells the story of Artemis, who, against her father's wishes, chose her own path and used her bow and arrow to aim at her goals in life. Artemis's story teaches girls that they can be independent and reach for the stars. Then comes the hugging exercise. Participants, both women and girls, pair up, and then one decides to be the person requesting the hug and the other the person being asked to be hugged. In front of the group, each pair does the exercise. The person asks something like, "Can I have a hug?" and the girl on the other end can choose to say yes or no. There is great power in letting girls know at an early age that they have the *right* to say *no*. Jamie of course teaches them that they should be polite and respectful in saying no, but that there is nothing wrong with not wanting someone to touch you if you do not feel comfortable or in the mood. The idea being that if a girl learns this now at an early age, it will be much easier for her to refuse an unwanted physical or sexual advance from a man or a woman later. As Jamie points out, this exercise is also important in helping build body memory. By practicing in safe spaces like a workshop or Red Tent, girls and women can consciously learn in a both a psychological and kinesthetic way so that when they encounter a situation that makes them feel uncomfortable their body and mind will respond appropriately.

Amy Jo Goddard, sexual empowerment coach and author of *Woman on Fire:*

> *"We violate the boundaries of small children when we make them hug adults. It starts there. It starts when we're very young, and certainly many girls go through sexual*

assaults and violations and abuse. There's so many ways that already, just by adolescence, we've learned that we don't get to have sovereign boundaries. It needs to be practiced. They need to understand how to set a boundary. They need to understand how to check in with themselves to figure out what their want is."

Jamie also highlights that consent can change and goes way beyond hugging:

"Boundaries and consent are a big issue. Consent can change. Just because you tell someone yes one time doesn't mean it's yes all the time, or yes the next time. It might be no the next time and then yes again. Something I'm working on personally is that consent of touching has now spilled over into other areas of my life where I'm really thinking about consenting to meetings, consenting to projects, consenting to my own thoughts in my head about myself. I think consent is really big deal, and we're not talking about consent with our girls hardly at all."

Jackie was eight years old when two high school boys raped her. Many years of healing work on her *own* boundaries allowed her to raise a daughter with healthy boundaries. Jackie believes that as mothers and women we have to question ourselves:

"How many times do I as a woman still say sorry? How many times do I as a woman still not say no when I mean

no? That's the core battle for ourselves, to say 'no' and where that line is is different for every woman. I think that part of the challenge is being able to hear yourself and learning to set boundaries. We need to help our daughters articulate what they feel from the beginning and helping them to learn to hear themselves. I think as mothers, we get scared of what maybe our daughters are saying so we try to change what they're saying and that is the first step of denying their truth and it happens when they're very young, and so to allow our daughters to say who they are regardless of whether we like it or not, I think, is the first step in giving them the tools to ultimately hear themselves."

We have to let our daughters hear their own voices and learn their own boundaries, but in order to really parent from a powerful place, we have to become an expert on ourselves. Self-Compassion and Mindfulness teacher and founder of HeartWorks, Kristy Arbon:

"Before we can help anybody else, including our own children, we need to do a lot of our own work. They say on the airplane, put your own oxygen mask on first, before you help those around you. I think that's the only way we can help teenage girls. If we can become an expert as a parent on our own body, our own intuition, our own sense of boundaries, and tend to our own emotional needs, we get a clearer picture of what's going on around us. We get a clearer picture of what's happening with our teenage girls."

Boundaries with Friends

An often underestimated element in arming your daughter against future trauma is teaching her mental boundaries such as how to defend themselves and others in an emotional/psychological capacity. Often the hardest people to stand up to are your friends. At any age, friends are important for long-term health and happiness, but for a teenage girl, close friends are almost like oxygen. While we know that friendships are important in a girl's life, we can sometimes underestimate the negative impact these friendships can have on a girl's self-esteem if the relationship sours. In *Finding Kind,* documentary filmmakers Lauren Paul and Molly Thompson highlight the ways girls can be abusive to one another and how scarring a friend's or a group of friends' betrayal can be. Being subjected to verbal or physical abuse by one's girlfriends and, worse, being rejected and isolated by friends can make a girl vulnerable to sexual abuse from a boy preying upon her loneliness and pretending to be her friend.

It's not surprising that so many of us survivors who never developed strong boundaries internalized our trauma and blamed ourselves. We never learned that much smaller infringements on our personalities, our appearance, etc. were not right and, as most children and teens do, without anyone there to speak up and acknowledge our pain, we then determined that the problem was not that other girls were being cruel, but there must be something wrong with us. *I must deserve this.* Gestalt therapist and parent Alison Stone offers an example of one of many ways in which parents can help girls learn to tap into their feelings of having a barrier crossed:

"Girls have to learn boundaries with girlfriends as well as boundaries with boys. You need to ask your questions such as, 'How did you feel when you had plans and then she changed it and did that? Or what stopped you from telling her you don't like that?'"

Rhonda Fleischer's Princess Warriors program arms girls against some of the most challenging aspects in our culture by teaching them emotional intelligence, the importance of social support, valuing courage and kindness over appearance, finding their own voice rather than just fitting in, and other key qualities. One of the many exercises in the Princess Warrior curriculum is learning how to stand up for oneself and others with kindness. Through group dialogue, practicing in real life, and reenactments, girls can learn better boundaries. For example, possible scenarios girls may act out might be something as mundane as a kid grabbing your toy at recess or the last pair of scissors during arts and crafts. The participants then brainstorm possible ways to solve the problem, as well as the least effective ways to solve the problem, e.g., screaming or punching the kid grabbing your toy. They then act out the most effective, positive way to handle the problem. Another scenario is standing up for a person you know or don't know. These scenarios give only a taste of this empowered leadership training that teaches girls not just the importance of helping strength the community, but also strengthen themselves. Such training can pay off down the road during the teenage years when bullying or verbal sexual harassment takes place.

There is no easy answer to help girls navigate the minefield of female friendships, but through conscious parenting and programs like Princess Warriors, girls can learn to stand up for themselves. Learning to stand strong can also pay off when they are placed in a situation where they are pressured to drink or take drugs. While teenagers still lack a fully developed prefrontal cortex, which controls impulsive behavior, nevertheless learning to control desire, aka self-discipline, as clinical psychologist and author of *The Talk: What Your Kids Need to Hear from You About Sex* Sharon Maxwell recommends, is also another effective way to prevent teen substance and alcohol abuse.

Girls also need to be taught to set up boundaries online. They have to be on the watch of course for adult predators posing as teens, but they also have to watch out for sexual predators their own age. They need to practice proper "netiquette" and let their peers know or an adult know if their boundaries are being crossed. Just as it is not okay for someone to touch you without your consent or make sexual or other insults, it is not okay for someone to insult or sexually harass you online.

Model Mama

Your mama actions speak louder than words. Your daughters will listen to you about boundaries, but one of the most effective strategies is modeling your protection of your own boundaries. Do *you* have a good grasp on saying no to things? Saying no to people? How is your self-discipline? Do you take care of yourself and say no (to yourself) to that second glass of wine or that processed piece of food that you know will later drain rather than rejuvenate you? Can you stand up for yourself? Do you have trouble with boundaries? Do you have a history of having your boundaries crossed? This doesn't mean you have to turn into a saint—the super-boundary-holding mama—but if you have struggled with boundaries, now is the time to get better with them. You also have to model what it feels like to be in a calm body and how to handle stress. As therapist Meg Tobin points out:

> *"If I'm in a calm body, then I'm taking care of business. I'm responsible for my own emotions. I'm not putting them on anyone around me to calm me down. I'm also passing on self-care to my kids and passing on the capacity to be grounded, and the clarity that comes with managing stress. Because remember, when we are activated in that fight-or-flight response, our frontal cortex goes offline, and our capacity for decision-making and choice of words. By virtue of the fact that we are looking at this in ourselves and managing our own selves, that inherently creates a safer environment for our kids than if we're completely oblivious to what our own struggles were, and just numb it out, right? Then they learn to numb it out, and not trust their own perceptions, not live in their bodies."*

Why Am I Posting This Sexy Photo on Instagram?

Developing a strong sense of self, or a core, is also crucial. Clearly, many elements go into what shapes a child's sense of self. Fulfilling a child's basic needs and mirroring consistent love and support are some of the elements, but another factor as a girl grows is making sure she learns that it is important to check in with her needs and wants in general and as they apply to sex and relationships. As Peggy Orenstein highlights in *Girls and Sex,* today's girls might show all the trappings of liberated, sexually empowered females by posting sexy pictures online and showing female bravado, but when interviewed, these girls often admit to feeling pressured to act sexy and many don't even know why they do it. They are not taught to ask for or satisfy their own sexual urges, and yet they are expected to live up to an unobtainable ideal where they are somehow sexy, but not like a whore; innocent, yet not like a prude.

Our culture trains women to please in order to be accepted, and this need to please continues, just in a different format: online. Rather than making a Snapchat decision and engaging in Instagram thinking, girls need to pause, check in with themselves, and ask, what are the consequences of posting this sexy picture of myself online? Am I posting this sexy picture because it truly gives me pleasure to do so, or am I just doing it to fit in?

Having a strong core, a sense of values, and a sense of boundaries extends to how intimate a girl wishes to be with a guy and how intimate she is with her own sexuality. Studies have shown that young women who know what their sexual limits are and how to think it through before the "heat of the moment" occurs have a better chance of protecting themselves. Does she know how to ask for what she needs sexually? Does she know that it is her right to be pleasured, not just to *give* pleasure? It goes back to teaching girls how to respect their physical boundaries and to deeply respect their own bodies.

Gina Martin, a licensed acupuncturist and leader of an earth-based women's group, stresses the importance of teaching girls at a very young age:

"To honor the temple that is their body and to feel like they have complete and total ownership over it is vital. One of the things that I always say in the first moon ceremony to young girls is that when they begin bleeding, what their body is saying to them is that they are capable of creating and bearing a child. But that also means they're entering into a realm of their own sexuality that means they have to understand energetically that when they have someone, particularly a male, they are inviting that person into them energetically, and that the first question they need to ask is if he deserves that. Does he deserve to be invited into your energy, into your body, into you? Which is a very different question than, 'What do I owe him?', or 'Will he like me if I don't?'"

Concrete Advice from Survivors and Experts

Meredith is a successful lawyer who has raised three daughters, and recounts her experience of being date raped in college:

"When I started dating older boys and going to fraternity parties, there was this assumption that it was going to be sexual. The first time I ever had sex was in a car with a fraternity boy who just simply overpowered me. That was really traumatic because my immediate response was 'I'm going to be pregnant,' until I got through my cycle and I

knew that I wasn't. I would say, one thing for girls to be aware of is that going out with older guys for whom sex is normal is a dangerous slope."

Like so many survivors, Meredith never learned appropriate boundaries and never had parents who helped foster her self-esteem.

"I didn't get steered to protect myself or to think of my body as sacred. I never remember any conversation about sex or about boundaries."

We may not be able to transform the rape culture overnight. But we can bolster our daughters with powerful messages to counteract what they're learning from the outside culture. Healer, coach, and creator of the Priestess Rising Program, Marin Bach-Antonson:

"We have to be the voice to introduce our girls to the whole idea that their body is sacred. Their yonis are a gateway. Their wombs are the chalice of their creativity and their femininity. To introduce this languaging is a very, very powerful, powerful thing. I think we can give this to our children. Even just to plant the seeds of those, you never know how that's going to unfold in them."

Unfortunately, there is no vaccine, no overnight quick fix solution to immunize your daughter against sexual violence, however, there is profound insight, wisdom, and value in creating a larger outer community of women outside of your immediate family to help your daughter. Alisa Starkweather, a leader for over 30 years in fostering women's leadership and founder of the Red Tent Temple Movement, explains the motivation behind the movement:

"We want this pure water for our daughters, but we're in a very toxified culture. I've always felt it's important to build the culture for women that you really want to have happen. How do we actually create a culture for ourselves and for the girls in which they would be so honored to become a woman? They would look at older women and hear their stories and they could hear even if they've been through things, they could know that they're not alone."

The fact is that whether we like it or not, once our girls start to become teenagers they will start to assert their independence—and they may not always wish to turn to us to discuss everything related to sex. We are doing our daughters a serious disservice if we leave it up to fate and pray that the sex education in their school will enough. As Naomi Wolf's book, *Promiscuities,* illustrates, instead of women, it's young boys who are initiating girls into sexuality. It is boys and the culture at large that are sending girls mixed messages and a distorted view on what it means to become a woman.

As a teenage mom at age 17 and having experienced her own sexual trauma at an earlier age, Alisa knew she wanted her daughter to have more support when she turned 13:

"My daughter was beautiful at this point. She was very large-breasted. She had her period at 11. Even though she was in middle school, she had teenage high school boys who knew her name and were catcalling and wanted to be with her. I was like, I have got to do something. She's totally at risk and she's totally naïve and open. If I don't do this, she's just going to enter this space as a big secret from me."

This is why Alisa, with the help of her greater community of women, created an official sexual rite of passage for her daughter:

"What's inspiring to me is my daughter's initiation. This idea that an agreement or a set of responsibility as a sexual being and the things she would do. A set of expectations that women would have of her as she entered that versus just not having a clue or not having any validation that she was a sexual being. I wanted my daughter to meet with who used to be called the sluts, the whores, the ones that had experienced something sexually traumatic."

Alisa gathered a group of 40 or so women, each bearing a gift symbolizing a piece of wisdom she wanted to share. A smaller group of women wrote down advice, guidance, and words of wisdom, and sealed them in a box with honey wax.

"She was told not to open it until she was actually ready to know these things, until she was ready to be sexual. Then

she could open it. It was a doctrine for her of what we expected of her if she was going to be sexual. If you are going to be sexual, these are the things that we as your women's community, as your mother, as people around you, these are the things that we expect you to be responsible for."

There was much more to her daughter's rite of passage, which lasted several days, but the essential thing was that she had an official recognition that she was entering a new stage in her life.

Alisa and other wise women talk about the importance of girls having *aunties,* actual aunts or women mentors who a girl can talk to when she is too embarrassed to talk to her mother or father. Alisa also has annual gatherings where girls can choose their mentor.

"I think initiations, they are demarcations for when there's one thing and then there's now another place. That sexual education, that needs to begin to happen. Sometimes it's better in a community setting where it isn't the parent embarrassing the shit out of the young person."

And this community is essential for them to know, even before they become teenagers, that their bodies are sacred. It's like another outer boundary to help them recognize their own. We need to foster a community where girls can meet with women they trust. Alisa recognizes that it can be very hard for mothers to let go of the fact that their little girl is no longer a *girl:* she is a young woman.

We know that we can't protect our daughters completely, but if something were to happen to them, if they are brought up surrounded by women who stand by them, there is much more likelihood that they will speak up. They will voice their trauma. Jamie Waggoner tells a heartbreaking story of how the daughter of one of her close friends was abused for years by the friend's husband. Jamie leads regular Red Tents and believes firmly that had her friend's daughter grown up in a community where she had ready access to hearing women's stories and wisdom, the trauma and the abuse would not have continued for so many years.

Although known for founding the Red Tent Movement or Red Tent Temple Movement, Alisa Starkweather has profound experience in trauma work, having spent years doing Shadow work and Predator work-the idea being that we all have that predator inside of us. Alisa emphasizes the importance of girls and women developing that predatory instinct. The sense of "being astutely and acutely aware of her surroundings," as she says. We can't teach our daughters this from a place of fear. We have to *help nurture* the wild self that Clarissa Pinkola Estés writes about in *Women Who Run with The Wolves*. Alisa Starkweather:

> *"Enough defense in our daughter for her to recognize a predator, enough sense of self-worth so she knows no one can hurt her. She can't be controlled. We've helped her to be a truth teller, we've helped her to know what shame is and what it isn't, and how to release herself from that."*

Aside from this powerful women community, it is also important to look at what the outer community is doing. Some progress is happening. The most successful programs at the high school level in preventing dating violence and rape are ones like the "Safe Dates" program, which is a 10-session curriculum addressing attitudes, social norms, and healthy relationship skills. Results showed that four years after participating in the program, students in the intervention group were significantly less likely to be victims or perpetrators of sexual violence. Another resource is the "Shifting Boundaries" program, which is a 6- to 10-week, school-based dating violence prevention strategy for middle school students that addresses policy and safety concerns in schools.

At the college level, programs that show promise in preventing date rape and other sexual crimes include the Green Dot Bystander Intervention program, an approach that uses bystanders and is built on the premise that violence can be measurably and systematically reduced within a community.

It is very important for parents to investigate how their daughter's middle or high school handles sex education and dating violence. Find out from other parents and former students what the general culture is like. How does the school handle student problems like eating disorders? What involvement does the PTA have in addressing sexual violence issues? Do the programs teach boys and young men about their role in perpetrating rape? Given that the culture still places much of the responsibility and blame on the victim, it is so important to find a progressive program that will teach teenagers a more evolved view not just on *preventing* rape but on learning what feeds into rape culture and how to combat it.

When interviewed, parents who've raised teens recommend teaming up with other parents and strategizing about how to handle the "hot spot" problematic areas such as teen drinking and driving, drinking and drugs, unchaperoned parties, etc. Effective strategies include developing a solid communication network with other parents. At the college level, enlist the support of "popular opinion leaders," as the Green Dot Bystander Intervention program recommends.

The *Finding Kind* documentary illustrated that female friendships are very important to girls' development, and that there are ways to foster healthier friendships. Teaching your daughter the value of sisterhood, where friends support and look out for each other, is another way to protect her. Sisterhood can also happen online. At the college level, the Girl Code movement is an anti-sexual assault organization whose mission is to teach women to become empowered bystanders, identifying at-risk women and taking action to stop a rape from happening.

It may sound obvious, but knowing your daughter's friends is important, too. This is where over-scheduling your kids and yourself can be detrimental. As *Simplicity Parenting* author Kim John Payne and other experts advise, kids need down time. If they are constantly running around from one after-school activity to another, it leaves less time for them to sit down at the dinner table with the family, less time to bond and do an activity together, or just *be* together. The same goes for parents.

In our society, where you are valued for greater productivity and for doing and doing and doing, you can become so busy that you don't have time to be with your kids. So how can you possibly develop a strong, bonding relationship?

Mama Tiger

Slowing down the schedule is also a way to promote greater awareness. Mindfulness training for teens is becoming more popular. Developing further your "mama tiger" eyes comes with doing your own mindfulness training. While learning to be more in the present moment will not change society's views on male and female relationships and won't end sexual violence overnight, it is essential to helping you pick up on your daughter's behavior. Becoming more aware of comments your daughter makes and even body language could help you better determine if she, for example, is being sexually harassed or if she is showing low self-esteem or other behaviors that could make her more susceptible to being sexually assaulted. It's like being a mama tiger very keyed into your daughter's every move. As Susan Ford Collins explains:

> *"Being in that position of asking questions or just listening or noticing that they're not quite the way they usually are. I think mothers have to be extremely into this because otherwise we miss the signals. Did they change the way they dress? Did they stop talking as much as they usually did? Do they seem sad? Do they spend more time in their room?"*

Safe Haven Mama Communication

I have never used and thought of the word *safe* in so many contexts until I dove headfirst into the world of sexual assault prevention and healing and raising strong daughters. The whole notion of *safe communication* or being a *safe* person for your daughter to talk to might seem like some airy-fairy construct that you read about in parenting books that sounds nice in theory, but doesn't directly point to a clear-cut way to protect your daughter. No, creating a safe space of communication does not equal full immunity from of life's evils for your daughter. However, as experienced moms explain, open communication lays a solid foundation that can allow your daughter to really own her power. Often, this starts by a child having her feelings validated, so she can own her feelings. As Marin Bach-Antonson explains, this can only happen if we shift our mindset:

> *"We live in a masculine culture that conditions us to fix, to fix, to fix. I don't feel good about myself, what should I do? Let me do yoga. Let me a do juice fast. Let me do a workshop. Let me fix, fix, fix these negative feelings because they're not okay. In speaking to our children, this is the biggest piece that so many mothers miss. They don't realize that they're not even doing it for themselves [validating their own feelings] so how can they possibly do it for their children? When your child comes to you and says, 'Mommy, I'm hurt' or 'Mommy, I had a terrible experience in school today,' the mother will often say, 'Okay. Here's what you need to do.' Fix, Fix, Fix. Rather than just say,*

and I've practiced this with my teenage daughter and it's miraculous, you mirror, 'Oh you had a hard day at school today.' You just sit and be with her. Your presence opens her up to feeling seen, to feeling heard, to feeling validated."

As Marin and others point out, if our daughters don't feel heard, if we immediately try to make them feel better or discount their feelings, they in turn learn that their feelings don't matter and that they shouldn't be feeling these negative feelings. On a certain level, they learn that *they* don't matter. If this repeatedly happens, you can see how, when sexual harassment or trauma occurs, they have been so conditioned to repress or negative their feelings that they may not even acknowledge that they are right to feel violated. They may also have learned that mom or dad is not only going to dismiss their feelings but criticize or condemn their behavior. The daughter learns that is not safe to talk them. She therefore has no one to bounce ideas off of, no one to reflect her pain or questioning.

Susan Ford Collins, best-selling author of *Our Children Are Watching* and expert on the habits of healthy, happy, successful people, explains how she overcame her dysfunctional family background and protected her two daughters while they were growing up.

"I was the go-to-person for my daughters and their friends whenever they were upset about something or they felt the boundary was being pushed. That allowed me to be there for them in ways that my mother and father had not been. Then I always encouraged full, open communication,

which meant that I was very neutral. In the family, I'm known as Switzerland. I allow people to know that they can come to me and they can tell me things and I that I will accept them and I won't betray anything."

Shaming Can Lead to More Shaming

Providing a safe space for your kids to talk means not shaming them. As Meg Tobin explains:

"We are very open with our kids. I have talked to my children from a very early age about sex, about sexuality, about their bodies. I interact with them in a way that opens the door for them to talk to me. So, I don't shame them. If they've done something crappy, I'll talk about how I'm disappointed in them. But I would never call them names. I would never shame them."

It is easy to see that if a child is shamed for minor misbehavior, she would start to internalize bad behavior as meaning *she* is bad, and then if she is ever placed in a situation where she is raped or sexually assaulted, how further shame is internalized.

When your daughter reaches a certain age, just discussing how she is dressing can be a minefield ready to explode at any moment—but you need to have that discussion nonetheless. As Alison Stone and other wise mamas and therapists point out, we don't want to slut shame our daughters and teach them that if they wear that pair of short shorts and get harassed, it is *their* fault. We don't want to put them in the "blame the victim" trap, but we have to acknowledge the complexities of the issues. Clinical psychologist Dr. Sharon Maxwell details the complexities:

"We are in the unfortunate position of having to explain to our daughters that although it is every person's responsibility to be in control of their sexual desire, everyone is not. In a culture where one in three teenage girls experience sexual violence, we have to teach our daughters to be prepared for the world as it is, and to speak out for the world they want to live in. As mothers we are always torn between wanting our daughters to embrace their sexuality and knowing the price they may pay if they try to do that."

As Dr. Maxwell recommends in her book The Talk, we need to teach our children that ultimately everyone is responsible for controlling and directing their sexual desire in a responsible and ethical way. However, everyone does not know how to do that. Therefore, we need to be aware that each of us has the ability to impact the sexual desire in a room, through our language, actions, and words. We should always be aware of how we are contributing to the sexual energy.

Another aspect of teaching your daughter how to protect herself is teaching her how to understand her own value. While learning meditation helps build awareness in the moment, self-awareness programs that also teach self-compassion can be very helpful. The mindfulness-based program, *Making Friends with Yourself,* which draws upon some of Dan Siegel's work on the teenage brain, is an excellent way to teach adolescents more about their stage of life so that they know they are not alone. Teens learn that the hormonal roller coaster and other pressures they are experiencing are normal.

Hundreds of Little Conversations
Psychotherapist Meg Tobin:

> *"I initiate a lot of conversations. Now, having a talk about sex ... that's a million brief moments of conversation. That's not 'The Talk,' right? So, I have been very aware of that for their entire lives. And the issues are different at different stages, and I get educated about what's appropriate at appropriate developmental points. And I meet them there. And so, I hold a space for them, because I allow them the room to be themselves."*

Media Cultural Boundaries
Even if we parents teach our children boundaries, Kristy Arbon explains that a teenage girl's sense of boundaries can start to become murkier as she starts to assert her independence by relying more on her peer's approval and that of the culture:

> *"We [adolescents] look to the culture as well to set boundaries. So, if the advertising is telling me I should look sexy, and I should wear particular clothes and I should be doing particular things, my sense of boundaries might still not be very safe, because I'm looking to culture to help me develop those things."*

Again, this is why giving a teenager unfiltered media access can be dangerous unless as parents and teachers, we have been able to teach them media literacy and gently nudge them to check in with themselves and see whether they are engaging in behavior just to please the culture, or for themselves.

However, when it comes to mainstream audiovisual media, you won't find Disney or the Hallmark channel teaching about how to prevent date rape. If it is addressed at all, it tends to glamorize or provide more shock value and simply perpetuate the violence against women by depicting it. While the Netflix series *13 Reasons Why*, a mystery unraveling the motives behind a high school student's suicide, paints the portrait of rape culture and offers a somewhat realistic glimpse into the "boys will be boys" attitude towards sexual assault, the question remains: What is the media doing to teach kids sexually responsible behavior?

Sexual responsibility doesn't sell very well. Besides critics and the media makers (how many are parents?) will say, "It's not the media's job to teach kids, it's up to the parents, or the teachers." Certainly, strong female role models and quality media exist to counteract sexual exploitation and violence, but the main driving force behind the marketing machine is not to uplift and make better citizens and happy, healthy humans, it's to make money.

Demonizing the media is not the answer, but letting kids have full license to unlimited media exposure is like sending a young warrior off to the battlefield before she has developed the muscles and brains to properly defend herself. It also goes against teaching kids the boundaries they need to protect themselves against their own impulses and those of others. As Sharon Maxwell explains, kids need to know their boundaries. Most well-meaning parents teach their kids all the anatomically correct names of the female and male genitalia and give biologically accurate accounts of sexual intercourse, pregnancy, and contraception, but what most parents fail to do is talk about the notion of the energy of sexual desire and also the entire principle of self-control—something rarely taught in our instant gratification consumer society. Our teens need to know how to handle desire for someone or something, whether it's a handsome boy or girl in a movie or a delicious piece of candy right before dinnertime, and the importance of discipline and controlling that desire. As Maxwell explains, it's important that we let teens know they are going to experience desire. Marin Bach-Antonson discuss with their teenage son and daughter the notion of desire and how confusing it can be:

> "We talk about how our body is a naturally burgeoning, hormonal landscape. When you start, your body is going to want part of this. It's going to feel good. It's going to be confusing. Your body might be saying one thing and your head is saying another thing. As much I can, I try to be honest and talk about all of it and allow her navigate and find her way. I think that children can—when you establish a sense that you trust them—they can trust themselves. The thing that we forget about our kids is that they have a perfectly designed intuitive mechanism inside of them. Oftentimes these bad decisions come from a place of needing something that they didn't get. They don't feel

seen by their parents. They want to feel seen by these boys.
They don't feel connected to their friends. They want to feel
connected, so they do drugs to feel connected."

Some parenting philosophies subscribe to completely eliminating media from a child's life, while other experts recommend limiting a child's media exposure. What Maxwell and other experts on teens and sexuality will agree on is, like it or not, even if you have sheltered your child from all technological and media influence and raised them somewhere in a remote idyllic countryside, unless you and your teen plan on spending the rest of your days in isolation, you are going to have to start talking to them about sex, and probably a hell of a lot earlier than you planned. Otherwise they are likely going to learn false or distorted lessons about sex, whether it's from intentionally or unintentionally stumbling across the wrong cable channel or surfing the Internet, hearing about sex from a friend whose parents let her have unlimited media access, or from an older sibling who decides to give them her version of "The Talk."

Parenting experts and studies show that when a child is exposed to media, it is important that parents know what they are watching and even watch certain TV shows or other media together as a family. Teaching media literacy is also key. Once they've reached a certain age, usually at the middle school stage, kids need to learn how advertising manipulates, how women are objectified in the media, and other ways the media can glorify aggressive sexual behavior towards women. Teaching kids at home as well as media literacy programs in schools have been shown to be effective in making girls more aware of sexting and sexual harassment.

Like any tool, the media can be a powerful tool if used wisely. There are progressive publications like *Teen Vogue* and online media sites such as Teen.com, GirlTalkHQ.com, Teenink.com, and others covering the issue of date rape and sexual assault, discussing ways teens can protect themselves, the ways teens can help take political action, etc. There are progressive social media sites that can provide a venue for teens to share safely. There are also ways to use media to interact with your daughter.

Sit down with her and watching her favorite TV show, then discuss the issues raised in the show. Know what media she is consuming. When she is at an appropriate age, watch films and documentaries with her that address serious issues from human trafficking in films like *Taken* to the exploitation of teenage girls in the international modeling industry in the documentary *Girl Model*. Joining or creating a mother/daughter book club is another way to select media that matters. It also makes it easier to talk about issues by talking about them through the characters.

Chapter 4
MIND GAMES

Realizing that a key component of protecting my daughter is being physically and mentally present—really being *there* for my kid—has forced me to face my finest ally but often my fiercest enemy: my mind. As I've started to take more time for myself and actually *slow down*—even if it means getting up a half hour before the rest of my family wakes—I've started to realize that for a long time, somewhere in the recesses of my mind, it's as if I've been running my life like a weary warrior who is no longer fit for battle, but won't put down her weapons and instead just keeps running (or, at this point, limping) away from the enemy. In my work with

47

women one of the first things I emphasize is learning to work *with* not against your mind.

We all need to protect ourselves. All warriors need their weapons. But all warriors also need rest. Unless you are in a war zone, you can put down your weapons. Slow down and sit still. Perhaps the hardest thing to accept is that the enemy you are running away from could be yourself: your inner critic, your worst memories, etc. One of the best ways to start facing your mind is to start noticing your thoughts and the many charades and tricks your mind plays on itself. Once you start becoming more aware of this, you can start channeling the energy that you once used negatively into positive mind games. But first, you have to sit still and start with some kind of meditation.

As the wellness scene becomes more mainstream and science continues to point to the mind/body connection and the toxic effects of stress, more and more people are learning about mindfulness and meditation. Loads of research points to the exponential benefits of consistent meditation. For those of us moms who are already hard on ourselves and feel like we aren't good enough, meditating becomes another self-improvement to-do and, when we don't do it, yet another reason to beat ourselves up.

For most of us, the ups and downs of life and the particular stresses of mamahood can push us toward distraction in an effort to escape our lives. For those of us who've experienced trauma, it is especially tempting to disappear into distraction and escape. That escape can take the form of continually staying busy, continually planning, traveling, various addictions, etc. I still struggle with a daily meditation practice, but I am reminded of the advice of Lama Surya Das, born Jeffrey Miller on Long Island, who despite his holy Buddhist new name has the quick-witted, no-nonsense humor of a New Yorker. As he points out, most of us are not living on top of a mountain in a monastery, able to meditate for hours on end. You can incorporate shorter, smaller nuggets of meditation into your daily life. He even talks about "spontaneous meditation." *Breathe, Mama, Breathe: 5-Minute Mindfulness for Busy Moms* and other books and blogs tell us, encouragingly, that we can be anywhere—in the driving lane picking up our kids from school or packing school lunches—and take a 60-second break. No matter how busy we are, we *all* can take five minutes or even one minute to sit, focus on our breath, and center ourselves.

Many find a more accessible mediation practice in loving-kindness, or Metta Meditation, which fits under the larger umbrella of mindful self-compassion, the idea of loving yourself even during times when you feel the least loveable or when life is the most challenging, just as you would a close friend or your daughter. This can be the hardest to practice when pain or suffering comes up, which is why the skill of mindful self-compassion must be practiced. Loving-kindness meditation is a tool to help access it. Kristy Arbon:

> *"It's not being judgmental towards ourselves. It's being present for ourselves even when we're not enjoying our experience, so not checking out, not abandoning oneself. It's giving ourselves kindness and love and physical support, so taking the time to stop and make ourselves a cup of tea when we're having a difficult time. Give ourselves the*

space that we need. All of the things a dear friend would
do for us, if we went to them and let them know we were
having a hard time."

When my kids were babies and toddlers and I was
exhausted—and now on days when I'm not feeling well—I
simply meditate by lying in bed placing my hand on my heart,
taking some deep cleansing breaths and practicing loving-
kindness. Years ago, I took a class with renowned American
Buddhist Sharon Salzberg. Choose a quiet place and, in an
ideal world, practice in the same spot each time so you can
program your mind and body to switch into meditation mode
when you sit down in that space. Close your eyes (unless you
are tired, in which case eyes open are fine) and start focusing
on your breath. You practice by closing your eyes and reciting
a few phrases, usually four. Saltzberg and others give four or
five sample phrases to start with but you can choose words and
phrases that resonate best with you. With Metta, the idea is to
first start practicing self-love, the idea being that if you can't
love yourself, you can't possibly fully love others:

Metta phrases:

May I be safe.
May I be healthy.
May I be happy.
May I live with ease of well-being.

After doing a couple of rounds of reciting the phrases
to yourself, you then think of a loved one—your daughter

or your husband or another family member—and practice directing your compassion toward them: "May Philip and Susan be safe. May Philip and Susan be healthy. May they be happy. May they have ease of well-being." Then, if you have time, practice saying these phrases while thinking of someone neutral, meaning someone you know superficially but interact with regularly, like the woman at the dry-cleaning store or the guy who serves you coffee. Next, if you are really ready to move on, you can practice Metta toward someone who you are really angry with or someone you hate. It could be someone who has really gotten under your skin. Finally, the goal is to practice Metta toward all beings.

When walking women through Metta, I always remind them that if they do not have energy to practice all five phases, they should at least practice Metta on themselves. It can be hard to think of ourselves when we give so much to our families and to others. We can feel depleted. And as trauma survivors and mothers, our reservoir for giving and for resilience is even further depleted. As therapist Meg Tobin and other trauma experts explain, trauma survivors often have a harder time managing stress if they have never fully dealt with the initial trauma. The feeling of being unsafe is locked inside our bodies. We have an underlying anxiety or stress in our systems and a smaller reservoir to take on further stress. This is why it is so incredibly important to be extra gentle with ourselves.

Imagining You Are Your Daughter Hack
When in doubt and finding it impossible to be loving to yourself, imagine how you would counsel your daughter if

she were having trouble meditating and taking care of herself. You would encourage her. You would be gentle and remind her how much she deserves to love herself and take time to nurture herself.

A Daily Practice, a Daily Choice

In working with women I remind them that there are many different ways to train and heal the mind, and meditation, like most practices, is best if it is becomes a daily practice. Training the mind is not an overnight process. It's also important to remember that *choice* plays a big role in your healing and in helping your daughter. Will you *choose* to be a worrying mama who will run herself ragged trying to raise the perfect daughter and protect her from all evils, or will you *choose* to be a healing, happy, strong mama? Sometimes we need some kind of life crisis or breakdown for us to wake up and decide we need to face our demons. For me, it was my moment inside the Red Tent that night, where a deeper part of me—perhaps my hurt, 15-year-old self—made the choice to face my demons. For Jennifer, who was sexually abused as a girl, the moment came years before she became a mother:

> *"I had a lot of suicidal thoughts and was hospitalized a few times because of that. At some point, in my mid-twenties, I woke up in the morning and I said, 'I'm done being a victim. I don't want my life to be like this anymore.' And it didn't miraculously change. I changed. My perspective changed. My intention changed. I'm deciding this isn't what I want. Somewhere along the way, somebody gave*

me the concept that I have a choice. And being an abuse
survivor, I never knew I had choice."

Motherhood: The Ultimate Way to Hide from Your Problems, or the Best Way to Face Your Problems?

The ultimate, most justifiable form of escape is motherhood itself. What better excuse do you have to stay busy as you run around being a super-mama, driving your kids to every possible fulfilling extracurricular activity, feeding them the most wholesome food possible, and raising a strong, confident daughter? By now you're probably starting to realize that in order to raise that kick-ass daughter, you're going to have to stop kicking your ass and calm your mind. Has your low self-esteem caused you to be perfectionistic in your parenting? Instead of beating yourself up for, well, beating yourself up about not being a perfect enough mom, how about being grateful for that perfectionist inside you who has pushed you to pick up this book and open up so you can protect your daughter and heal yourself?

Britney was 14 when her male school teacher sexually assaulted her. For her, at first, motherhood was an escape:

"Motherhood took me so far from myself that I almost
couldn't remember anything prior to the birth of my
daughter. As she got older, I strived to keep her safe. It's easy
to fall into the day-to-day caretaking of a child so that you
bury what happened to you. Then, when you least expect
it, it comes back to the forefront, and you can't devote time
and energy to it because you have a little child to care for."

Perhaps you've turned yourself into a mama martyr where for what seemed like an eternity of sleep deprivation—five or six years maybe—you escaped your problems. But as the school years approached and the prospect of teenage years beckoned, your own suffering as a teen has resurfaced. By learning the tricks of the trade from mamas who have been down that road before, you have started to realize that you can't protect your daughter if you are not fully present in your body and in your mind.

For many of us survivors, the disconnection is from our bodies and our feelings. Early healing can mean getting back in touch with our feelings. Britney:

"Early in my therapy, I didn't know how to identify a feeling. I could tell my therapist what I thought, but not what I felt. We worked with guided meditation and visualization to uncover feelings. She would walk me through going down a ladder into an igloo, which was my safe zone. I could feel there, and talk to her about the feelings, and when I came out of the igloo, I could go back to 'thinking' until next time I was in the igloo. Eventually I was able to feel outside of the igloo. Now, I think I sometimes take things too personally and my feelings are hurt about things that are not personal. I am a work in progress."

Red Tent Mindset

For me, the ultimate healing moment came inside a Red Tent. The womb-like comforting yet sensual vibe of the surroundings felt incredibly safe for me. But clearly we can't spend all our days inside a Red Tent. How can we carry this feeling inside our minds? We need to create a Red Tent-like mindset where we create a safe place inside ourselves. Visualizing an imaginary or real physical space, whether it's a beautiful beach or lake side you have visited or your favorite reading nook in your current or former home, can help you create that inner safe, cozy place where no invader can come in. When you are imagining this space, make sure that all the soothing colors you love are in there. Images of nature help.

As with visualization techniques that Olympic athletes and others use, it is best if you incorporate as many senses as possible. Is it a warm spring day, or are you inside a cozy room at night? Do you smell anything that is appealing and soothing to you? Do you hear gentle music or the sound of birds or crickets in the background? Are your bare feet touching the sand, or are you surrounded by soft blankets and plush carpets? Whatever it is, start to visualize this image.

First you can do this visualization technique at home in a quiet spot and imagine yourself feeling, breathing, and seeing safety all around you. At first you may need to imagine that you are inside a bulletproof Wonder-Woman–like invisible airplane where no one can hurt you, where no one can see you, and you are free and safe. As you get used to visualizing this image at home in a state of quiet and calm, you can call upon this image when you out in the world driving or doing errands or at work. To help remind yourself of this image of safety, you can draw a small image of it and carry it with you in your purse, or print out a picture of a similar scene of nature from the Internet or screen save an image for your cell phone or desktop. These are tricks to remind yourself to stay in the conversation of how you can feel safe and strong. For more in-depth exercises that incorporate visualization and other techniques to help you feel safe, deal with lingering feelings of unworthiness or shame, and help you feel more resilient about handling life's stresses, I have found the website of Linda Graham, a psychotherapist trained in mindfulness, to be an excellent resource for recorded exercises. I often like to use these guided visualizations as well as my own when in circle with other women.

Mantras

Sometime picking an inspirational phrase or even one word to recite to yourself as you go about your day can be very helpful. The key is that it has to be something that truly lights you up and that feels authentic to you. As with guided imagery and visualization, reinforce the mantra using at least a couple of your senses to help strengthen its message. Just as teachers will incorporate kinesthetic (physical) learning to help reinforce their teachings, another way to help mantras seep into your psyche is by practicing power poses like the ones that gained popularity through psychologist and Harvard professor Amy Cuddy's 2012 TED talk and were confirmed by at least nine other published studies. Power poses are universal body postures (hands on your hips like Wonder Woman or hands in the air in victory) that elicit neurological and physical sensations of truly feeling powerful. I'll cover more of this in Chapter Six: The Body Temple. Practicing powerful yoga poses also work well with a mantra.

In co-leading women's circles, I have found putting pen to paper is another way of shining light on an otherwise ignored, dormant issue. Sitting down to meditate may not always appeal to you. If this is the case, writing down your thoughts and feelings, however chaotic or mundane they may be, has been scientifically proven to heal your brain *and* your body, as *Opening Up* author James W. Pennebaker demonstrates in several of his renowned studies. For years, I heard about people who journaled, but I dismissed it as something that sounded like a nice thing to do, but that was not very powerful. Then I read *Writing Down Your Soul* by Janet Connor and *Opening Up,* and learned there was scientific proof of people healing through writing. As I began to write every morning before my kids woke up, I started to notice how much more present I was when I greeted them in morning. It was as if I had meditated. It was an effective way to declutter my mind and process my whirlwind thoughts and emotions. While specific journal writing as prescribed in *Opening Up* and *Writing Down Your Soul* is very effective, *any* kind of free form journaling about your emotions regarding your trauma and the flurry of thoughts whirling around in your mind can be helpful. For Jennifer, journal writing was tremendously healing:

"I wrote a lot. Journaling was a real saving grace for me. Twenty years or so ago, I had volumes and volumes of journaling about my trauma. Some friends of mine and I got together and we had a bonfire and we burned them all. I kept holding onto them, thinking, 'Maybe if I write a book someday.' And I thought, 'You know what? When I need to remember, I'll remember. If I ever

want to write a book, this is not something I'm going to easily forget.' As time goes by and I have lost a visceral connection to the stories, I don't remember many of the details anymore. And I'm glad. Because that means, it's not in my body anymore."

For some survivors, writing is the ultimate form of healing. Cea Sunrise Person is the best-selling author of *North of Normal* and *Nearly Normal,* both memoirs chronicling her unconventional childhood living in the Canadian wilderness and being raised by a dysfunctional, countercultural family. When interviewed about her biggest sexual trauma she had to heal from Cea explained:

"I've had many experiences with this as a child, but the most significant sexual trauma I've had was being molested by my mother's boyfriend when I was eight. He made me touch him instead of vice versa, which made me feel I was complicit in the exchange for decades. Also, my mother knew what was happening but didn't try to stop it because she didn't really see anything wrong with it. She was sexualized from a young age and thought it was okay for me to be as well. I wrote two memoirs about my life and included all the sexual abuse incidents in them. Writing about them helped me much more than any therapy ever did."

While therapy can be life changing, some people argue that after a certain point you can get stuck in a kind of healing plateau by telling your story over and over again. Others argue that going over your trauma over and over can be re-traumatizing. This is why alternative practitioners, healers, and many survivors, including myself, swear by EFT (Emotional Freedom Technique), otherwise known as tapping. Basically, you use your fingers and tap specific meridian points on your body and face while saying a specific phrase out loud about what is emotionally charged or disturbing to you. The theory is that the tapping mechanism helps your brain and body fully process the emotions in a way that regular talk therapy does not.

For other survivors, a huge part of their healing lies in their artistic expression. Jackie:

"Theater was the first real healing place for me where I could use someone else's story to express my pain and my rage. I found that I was doing a lot of scenes in acting class that gave me the space to bring that secret without ever having to tell anyone outright and work with the feelings of that experience, so it was a secret I kept bringing into my work as an actress over and over again. I ended up writing a one-act play that was again masked with fiction. That was the first time I came out with my story, but no one knew that's what I was doing, so it remained a secret. But it was very healing for me to be able to put it into a story that I then watched other actors perform in front of me and in front of an audience, so it was really this giving voice to my story. I've continued to do that. I then became a filmmaker, and all of my films have addressed that trauma and then the healing from that trauma in

one way or another, and they've all been fictionalized so that my psyche felt safe to tell the truth each time I voice my story. The biggest healing for me has been in making art, giving voice to my story through art, be it acting or playwriting or filmmaking."

Chapter 5
SISTERHOOD

For some, the word sisterhood might conjure up images of naked women dancing around a fire (maybe not such a bad thing until you try it? Something to put on the bucket list?) and/or women who float around their daily existence calling every female sister and loving everyone. While I believe there are some individuals out there, past and present, who have done such an intense amount of healing and inner work that they really feel a sense of love and gratitude for every being, the rest of us still have our egos and our particular likes and dislikes. Sisterhood does not mean you have to like every woman you meet, but you could try respecting them. When did it become accepted in the common culture that women are catty? That we all gossip about one another? That we are so hard on one another? If there was equal pay for equal work, if women held at least half of all political positions and CEO jobs, if women were valued first for their minds and souls rather than their beauty—basically if women were not suppressed—would they feel this negativity, this self-hatred, and this need to tear their sisters down?

Without dwelling on cultural causes and blaming the patriarchy, how about we stop putting ourselves and our sisters down and stop reinforcing the stereotype? What if we as women were to start propping each other up more, and when we think something negative about another woman, we hold our tongues? This taps into the abundance mindset rather than having a scarcity mindset. At a young age, we learn a scarcity mindset, such as the teacher will only give out so many As, there are only four spots on the basketball team, only a select few students get into Harvard. And as we become women, it appears that only a select few make it to positions of leadership. We have the mindset that there are only so many pieces of the pie, so we had better look out for ourselves and watch out that another woman doesn't take our place.

After Priestess training with Marin Bach-Antonson, where I learned to lead women's circles, I have experienced firsthand what economists and thinkers like Franklin Covey, Oprah Winfrey and many other successful open-minded men and women have shown: when you shift to an abundance mindset where you believe there are plenty of pieces of pie to go around, your life will dramatically improve. In fact, by practicing gratitude, helping others, looking for the positive in situations and in other people, etc., you will start to create more and more abundant opportunities in whatever area you wish to improve in your life. It may seem like such an insignificant act, but even starting to talk more positively about the women in your own community and in your online community could very well have a snowball effect, causing more and more women to feel better about themselves, to support one another to give each other strength and support, and make women feel better about being women.

Maybe there is a scientific reason why sisterly betrayal, why pitting women against women, feels disturbing right down to our bones and right down to our cells. Considering the emerging research on cellular epigenetics, it is no longer such a stretch to suggest that sisterhood is rooted in our bones and that our DNA is not only hardwired for human connection, but also *sisterly* connection.

Perhaps it is less sisterly conflict, but more sisterly disconnection that so many women find profoundly painful. Some of the oldest religions pre-Christianity worshiped the goddess, mother nature, etc. Some cultures were matrilineal; land was passed down from mother to daughter, and to this day there are at least six different cultures around the world, from the Mosuo people in South West China to the Bribri people of Costa Rica, where land ownership is still passed down mother to daughter.

Throughout history in cultures all over the world, women held spiritual positions of power with such titles as priestesses, shamans, or the temple dancers of India. They were clearly leading the charge. I imagine egos, greed, and conflicts existed. It was not all *kumbayah* peace and love all the time, but women's strength and power was revered and allowed to flourish. Even in non-matriarchal cultures, sisterhood was promoted. All over the world in ancient cultures, life was more communal. Women cooked together, gathered food together, and took care of each other's children.

And in many cultures, the existence of the Red Tent was a powerful symbol of sisterhood. Since life was much more communal, women typically menstruated together and spent their moon time together in a hut or a tent-like structure where they would relax, talk, and celebrate major rites of passage, like a girl's first menstruation or a woman finishing menopause. While there have always been women's communities and groups, whether sewing circles or quilting groups or church groups, the Red Tent appears to encompass the most holistic coming together of womanhood: bonding together and openly venerating a woman's most intimate and unique aspect, her ability to give birth. The Red Tent not only represents the ultimate in sisterhood, it also mirrors the sensuality and voluptuousness of the female vulva with its folds and lips and warm, inviting, womb-like feel.

When female friendships run deep, they can be some of the most rewarding, satisfying relationships a woman will ever have. And sisterhood takes friendship to a whole new level. It is the notion that instead of just having one or two close friends and/or a small posse of friends and then distrusting everyone else, you can still have your closest friends and posse *and* also join a larger tribe of women whom you can rely on and trust implicitly as a form of support. This support can be like a cradle to nurture you as a mother. The support is like a giant safety net to catch you when you feel like you may fall into the abyss of isolation, depression, or anger. The way I learned of this kind of sacred sisterhood was through joining a circle first led by Marin Bach-Antonson:

> *"Sisterhood is this beautiful holographic experience in that we see ourselves in others and, again, through her story, you claim your own. Through her healing ... and this the other beautiful thing about sisterhood. When one woman heals in the circle, she truly raises the vibration for all of the women to experience some level of that same healing. The first thing about coming together in sacred circle is it connects to the divine. The second piece is back to the truth. When you begin to tell the truth to yourself, that is one level of healing. When you begin to tell your truth and you are witnessed by a circle of women who are there to say, 'We see you, we honor you, we love you,' that has incredible healing potential."*

A circle is an ancient tradition where women gather together and honor themselves. As Marin Bach-Antonson explains in her Priestess e-books and trainings, you do not have to be Pagan or Wiccan to believe in the idea of the Goddess, another word for the feminine energy, and gathering together in a circle. One key element of a circle is gathering around, seated on the floor, and having some kind of talking stick, which doesn't even have to be a stick but can be any kind of meaningful object to the group that, when held by the person ready to talk, means that everyone else in the group must listen without interjecting comments or advice, no matter how helpful the listeners think it is. Having a talking stick allows the participants to truly experience what it means to practice profound listening and the speaker to experience what it means to be truly heard. If a person wishes to receive advice, then they can ask for it. We all have the masculine "doing" type energy and feminine "being" energy, or yin/yang, inside of us, but because we live in a culture where the masculine is more valued, we often exhaust our masculine energy and neglect our feminine. The idea of the circle is to create an atmosphere with scent, sight, sound, e.g., an altar in the center of the circle with flowers, candles, and incense, along with softly dimmed lights and gentle music to create a feeling that fosters the feminine energy.

Jackie:

"I think the most powerful part of sisterhood is being heard and being mirrored. As sisters we know when a sister speaks through grief or her rage, I get it. When I speak mine, she gets it, and we feel less alone in the world and you feel less crazy. There is a way in which living as a woman who's been sexually traumatized in this society you can feel very isolated. Society makes you feel wrong and crazy, and this is the society that blames the victim. It's scary to speak our truth in a society that will immediately tell you you're wrong about your experience, you're lying about your experience. To be able to gather with other women

*who can actually hear your experience, can reflect back
your experience, and can say, 'Yes, I hear you. I honor and
validate your truth,' that's I think the most healing thing."*

For many women, survivors of sexual assault or not, having
the approval of our female friends is still important. Often as
rape survivors our self-esteem is low, therefore developing the
habit of loving ourselves is very challenging. One of the best
tools or hacks to practicing self-love is forming a group or circle
of supportive women who will hold you accountable in a firm
yet loving way to loving yourself and to *not* putting yourself
down. Sometimes the mere act of being listened to and hearing
yourself berate yourself or be hard on yourself is enough.
But sometimes it is hearing your circle sister remind you of
everything you stand for or tell you what she loves about you
that can keep you on track to greater self-loving. Sister mamas
act like a mirror, reflecting back to you your inner strength,
inner beauty, and goodness.

Leanne, who was date raped in college, found that joining
a women's circle a couple of years later put her on the path to
faster healing:

*"I felt such shame and self-hatred that it took me a long
time before I could practice love toward myself. But I found
it much easier to [feel] compassion and love the women in
my circle. The more we shared our stories, the more my
heart opened up. These women were like soul sisters who
supported me through everything and completely accepted
me, and I realized that they were no different than me. If I*

*could show them the same deep sisterly love, why shouldn't
I give myself this same level of love and respect?*

*"I had started therapy, which was where I was finally
able to say the word 'rape' and acknowledge that I had
been raped, but it was only when I started experiencing
the love and healing power of a circle of women that I
began to really open up. Hearing other women tell their
stories of pain—some sexual trauma, some just deep shame
about their bodies—made me realize that I was not alone
and that I had the right to feel angry and I deserved so
much better in my life."*

To this day my doubting mind—the agnostic part of
me who was taught that so-called concrete science trumped
anything magical or intangible—still questions whether spirits
exist. For years, I have attended circles and heard Priestesses like
Marin Bach-Antonson acknowledge the spirits and ancestors in
the room, and there would be a part of me that would not fully
embrace it. Yet almost every woman I have talked to who has
done a lot of healing work and is living a rich, full happy life
will tell you that when you circle powerfully with other women,
the room is full. Amy Jo Goddard:

*"When we're in circle with women who've come to heal
their sexuality, the room is always very full. They come.
Spirits, ancestors, they all show up. All these women come
in, and it's not just them. They're bringing in all their
ancestors who didn't get to do the healing work and who
are also there to do the healing work. It's just not all about*

the personal. Sometimes it's about healing something ancestral, in our maternal line or our paternal line, we're doing that healing for our families."

To appease the doubter or the inner critic, I remind myself of the emerging science around cellular memory and epigenetics, and that pretending that my ancestors are in the room can be a beneficial psychological exercise. However, as I reread Clarissa Pinkola Estés *Women Who Run with the Wolves* and as I enter mid-life, I realize I don't need to have proof of ancestors in the room when I circle. When I have my doubting moments, I will use the tricks of patriarchy to lull my inner critic to sleep. I don't have to fully believe in order to reap the luscious benefits of swimming in circle sisterhood.

While less intimate than a small circle, experiencing the power of hundreds of supportive women coming together forming a kind of giant safe cocoon within at a women's festival such as Where Womyn Gather is way to jumpstart your connection to sisterhood. Another very positive aspect of attending a women's festival is that it gives you the opportunity to meet older women, wise women who are at the crone stage of their lives, meaning they have finished menopause, are entering the last third of their lives, and see the world in a different light now. It is also a way to at least temporarily silence the inner critic. It was here that I attended Elizabeth Nahum's *Clearing the Motherline*. Nahum is a wise crone healing practitioner with academic and alternative training in victimology, energy work, and other disciplines. In her workshop, Nahum uses shamanic journeying to release traumas never healed from your ancestors and help you reclaim your inner power. You have to experience it to fully understand it, but even if you question the notion of an *ancestral curse* or that your great-great-great-great grandmother's unhealed trauma is affecting you, when you experience this deep shamanic training, it can unleash pain you never knew you had within you.

Long before I became aware of women's issues, I had seen pictures and artwork of harems. Long before I realized that harems were basically enslaved women forced to be of service to men, I was drawn to the images of women dressed in sexy, sensual clothing and relaxing in a sensual environment with cushions, soft fabrics, and lounge chairs. This is why I find the Red Tent environment so appealing, because there is a freedom for women to lounge around, to fully relax, to feel sensual and yet safe. Throughout history, women haven't been able to appear in a public space free to wear what they choose, to uncross their legs, to lie down and relax, to express themselves however they wish without being open to the scrutiny, the dominance, and the violence of men.

Amy Jo Goddard:

"Women really need spaces away from the patriarchy where they can do their healing work, where they can be free of the male gaze, of the gender dynamics that women can get very tripped up in. Not that there's not dynamics among women. Of course there are as well, but I think that when women can come together and be in a space that is held very carefully and where containers are really strong so that women are free to do their work and to really

be witnessed by other women and held by other women, it is just beyond valuable, it's extremely powerful."

In working with women and especially mothers, I have found that having a circle of moms can be extremely helpful in supporting one another while parenting. We give so much as mothers that we need to remind each other to give to ourselves and to give to each other as mama friends. We can also support one another in our parenting by listening to each other's stresses and, if called, by offering each other advice and support on the best solutions to the many challenges that arise. Often the support is less about specific tips on how to raise a child and more about taking care of ourselves as mamas.

As you start to reap what you give to your circle of female friends and it creates more feelings of love and generosity the love builds upon itself. You start to feel better about yourself as a friend, a mama, and a person.

Chapter 6

THE BODY TEMPLE

For some women, childbirth is yet another traumatizing event, another sacred rite of passage over which they have no free will—especially in the United States, where the patriarchal medical model presents mothers as quasi-fragile, inferior beings and the doctors, *not* the birth mothers, are in control. However, if a woman has had a chance to work on her own healing before giving birth, the act of childbirth can go from being traumatizing to virtually transforming. The healing journey for me is far from over, but thankfully I began therapy and other healing work in my twenties.

Part of this work led me to join women's groups and meet women activists and leaders such as author Naomi Wolf who wrote *Misconceptions: Truth, Lies, and the Unexpected on the Journey to Motherhood.* I ended up working as a researcher for Naomi at the end of her writing of *Misconceptions.* This experience led me to homebirth both my children and reclaim part of myself that was lost as an adolescent and orchestrate this sacred rite of passage by having my husband by my side and by choosing a couple of wise women—my midwife and a birthing doula—to help me birth my babies. In giving birth, I realized how the trauma had affected me in that I needed my doula to remind me repeatedly, "*You are strong. Y*ou are strong." Having had so much power taken away without my consent and being told in so many ways by the culture at large that I was a woman and therefore weak, I needed to hear that I was indeed a *strong woman.*

For Jackie, childbirth was also challenging and healing at the same time:

"In the middle of my birth I was having flashbacks to my rape, and I just started with my whole body, the contractions became about getting those boys off of me, and I was literally shouting at the top of my lungs, 'Get the fuck off of me! You can't have this, this is mine.' Over and over, it was like the pushing, the contractions were just pushing these boys off my body and reclaiming my body. It was a huge epic healing for me."

For many of us who have experienced abuse, our relationship with our bodies is far from being a positive one. For some women survivors, their pain transforms into overeating or alcohol or drug abuse, while others develop anorexia or bulimia to block their pain. Jennifer describes the way she coped with her childhood sexual abuse:

"What happened to me when I was younger was I pushed it down out of my consciousness. And the way it showed up for me was as a pretty severe eating disorder: anorexia and bulimia. The truth was, I was grieving. I was angry. I was full of rage that I tamped down. I was the good girl who did everything right, who never made a conflict, who never spoke up for herself. I was who you wanted me to be."

In co-leading women's circles I have found for many women, there is still the feeling of being completely disconnected from one's body. The temple that was once sacred is a place you no longer treat with reverence, you neglect and rarely acknowledge it. For me, feeling completely disconnected from my body was my biggest issue in my twenties and well into my thirties. I prided myself on being able to eat anything and not caring about dieting, when the reality was that I had a deep-seated shame about my body that had been violated. I was never taught to trust and revere my body, and after the ultimate in violation, I distrusted it completely. My distrust and anger manifested as cold, hard indifference masking as irreverence. Yet as Kristy

Arbon explains, even women who have not experienced sexual trauma learn at a young age to ignore and devalue their body, and this is partly a cultural phenomenon:

> *"In our Western culture, we tend to not be encouraged to listen to our body, we tend to sort of be dissociated from our body, the emphasis is on what our mind, what our brain can do, the whole 'mind over matter, mind over body' concept."*

For most girls and women, the word temple does not even figure into their own education òf their bodies. Given the thriving princess industry, perhaps it's more appropriate to use the word "castle" to explain the way girls learn about their bodies. It is paradoxical, in a way, that girls learn at an early age to spend a great deal of effort to make the exterior of their castle beautiful, shiny, glittery, sparkly and very inviting, yet inside the foundation is weak, the fortress is easily penetrable, and without male guards to protect it, the castle will come tumbling down. The bright, pretty, flimsy castle lies open to be easily invaded and then saved by a prince in order to take it over and reign over it. The princess never learns to master the building and maintaining of the castle. She stops listening to the sounds of disrepair within the castle walls or the cries from the birds or other animals warning her that something is awry.

Since we are taught to value our mind over our bodies, we lose sight of when our physical boundaries are crossed. As Kristy Arbon explains, we forget our internal wisdom:

"We get these messages from our body about things like boundaries, like when something happens in our environment. We might have a subtle sense of unease about something. If we've never been taught or encouraged to listen to these messages from our body, and to see these as warning signs, 'Hey a boundary has just been stepped over,' or 'Someone's getting close to stepping over a boundary,' or 'I'm getting close to stepping over my own boundary'— if we never learn to tune into that sense of intuition, that internal wisdom this is emergent self-wisdom, we actually have in every single moment. If we're not taught to listen to that, then it's really hard to establish authentic boundaries."

For many sexual abuse survivors, there is fear that the temple will once again be invaded. When we have been violated, especially as children or teenagers, often our fight, flight or freeze mechanism—our body's way of protecting us by allowing us either to fight back, to escape quickly, or hide (freeze) in an emergency—is on overdrive. For many of us, it is as if our body thinks that we are constantly in danger, especially during moments of stress. As we age, it can get harder to manage stress, and parenting, with all of its rewarding moments, is also very stressful for anyone. Now combine trauma, a reduced ability to handle stress, and the stress of parenting an adolescent girl, and you have a perfect storm of factors pushing the stress situation to red alert. As therapist Meg Tobin explains, it is very important for survivors to have more experiences of feeling safe in their bodies.

"If we could live in a calm body, then we can learn that there is now safety in the world. We can learn that every man is not a predator. We can learn that our children have the possibility of being safe. We can learn what the current reality is, as opposed to what our perception of it is based on our past case for learning, and it all stems from a calm body."

Before we can even begin to experience what life is like living once again in a calm body, we have to first start fully residing inside our temple not as prisoners but as devotees to its most sacred building. Changing our languaging and imagery around our bodies is paramount to healing. As Japanese researcher Dr. Masaru Emoto showed with his water molecule experiment featured in the film *What the Bleep Do We Know,* our intentions and our use of positive or negative words have a physical impact. By merely thinking of your body as a temple and creating an intention to honor it, you are planting the seeds to healing.

I like to walk women through gaining deeper awareness about how we as women talk to ourselves and our bodies. Our negative languaging about ourselves can be so deep seated, so insidious, that we have to be aware when it comes, such as when we catch ourselves looking in the mirror and instantly putting our bodies down. If you would probably never let your good friend or your daughter ever speak poorly about her body or herself in general, then please try to be gentle and don't speak that way to yourself. Consciously or subconsciously, your daughter is observing what self-love looks like in action from her first female role model: you. By modeling the importance of valuing your sacred female self with all its imperfections, you are showing your daughter how to value every inch of herself from her skin to her inner core.

Cultivating the worship and love of your body temple often starts first with practicing modalities that help you develop body awareness. Meditation, EMDR or Eye Movement Desensitization and Reprocessing therapy, deep breathing work, and other modalities tie in the mind/body connection. As Alisa Starkweather and other leaders in helping women heal will tell you, there are multiple levels and dimensions to doing deep breath work. However, to start off, learning basic breath work is helpful. As you focus on your breath, you become aware of the tension in your body or something positive in your body. In mindfulness training, a popular exercise is the body scan. In short, you focus on each part of your body, usually starting with your toes up to your head, slowly noticing how each part feels: whether it's cold, hot, stiff, tense, relaxed, numb, etc. Focusing on the body at times of emotional stress, whether happy or sad, is also an excellent way to practice awareness and learn to be in your body. Many of us, regardless of whether or not we have experienced trauma, tend to check out of our bodies when something stressful happens. Our regular pattern of emotional reactions starts racing around in our minds depending on what the triggers are.

Awareness of how we talk about our bodies is important, but listening to what our bodies are trying to tell us is perhaps more so. You may not even feel you are anxious, but your body feels it. Different scientific studies have shown that the body is more responsive or intuitive than the brain in picking up on information. One study, in which participants were given two different sets of cards—one loaded with higher number cards and the other with lower number cards—and hooked up to heart monitors and other equipment checking for sweaty palms and so forth showed that participants' bodies picked up on something awry with the cards long before the brain registered something was wrong.

If we fail to listen to our body, eventually our body will force us to pay attention. As the late motivational author Louise Hay outlined in her book, *You can Heal Your Life,* and as Dr. Christiane Northrup describes in *Women's Bodies, Women's Wisdom*, often women's reproductive maladies stem from sexual trauma. We have to listen to the body and also experiment with at least a couple of complementary practices to make significant progress in our healing. Most of us mamas on the healing journey as well as trauma experts such as Dr. Bessel Van der Kolk, author of *The Body Keeps Score: Brain, Mind and Body in the Healing of Trauma,* credit powerful trauma healing to a merging of at least two or three different kinds of treatment, one of which *always* involves the body. Neurofeedback, EMDR therapy, and yoga are examples of different ways to heal.

Incorporating several kinds of therapies, exercise, and body-centered work speeds up the healing. As Gestalt therapist Alison Stone explains, it is not one size fits all:

> *"For my clients, the more modalities they are doing, if they are meditating, if they are going to yoga, if they are doing other things, the therapy goes faster."*

While it took a number of years, Jennifer attributes her deeper healing to body centered therapy and using a variety of methods:

"I was blessed with some incredibly amazing and talented, gifted therapists who did body-centered work. And I feel like if I had been in therapy with just a cognitive practitioner, it would have been a lot longer of a journey for me."

Listening to the body is very effective in helping learn boundaries you never knew how to uphold when you were younger. As Alison Stone explains:

"Gestalt therapy is holistic therapy. We work with the body, we work with the breath. We work with what you are experiencing with the idea that our bodies and ourselves have the wisdom. I might ask a question like, 'How was that for you when you asked him to leave and he didn't leave?', but my goal isn't to tell people what their boundaries should be. It's to help them experience what they are comfortable with and the ways they may shut down awareness. Do they shut down awareness when they know they are not comfortable? When they think there's nothing they can do about it so they will just go numb? Or did they shut down awareness earlier before they even realized they were being violated and just feel off without really knowing what it was all about?"

For the first fifty years of her life, Beth suffered from chronic depression and felt dissociated from her body. It was only until she tried EMDR therapy that she was able to fully process her father molesting her at age nine. As Beth explains:

"The EMDR brought me back into my body. Most of my life I was probably not living inside my body. It was always like there was this little 'mini me' sitting on my shoulder where I couldn't see it. It was just out of my vision. It was a little mini me watching the world and interacting with the world."

It was only during a counseling training program with a group of people with whom she felt very safe, having worked closely with them for a couple of years, that Beth experienced a flashback to a memory of being a girl wrapped up in blankets in a corner, afraid of her father coming into her bedroom:

"I felt myself leave my body and sit behind myself in that corner. It was me as a little kid, all crumpled up with my knees clutched to my chest. I was able to verbalize, this is what was going on, and it scared me to death. I knew it happened. My trainer then recommended EMDR."

EMDR first gained popularity for its effective treatment of war veterans suffering from PTSD (Post Traumatic Stress Disorder) and is now used to treat rape survivors' PTSD symptoms. The theory is that rapidly moving your eyes back and forth and following the lead of a therapist while talking about a traumatic event will lessen its emotional and psychological impact on you. The particular movement of the eyes back and forth mimics the same process of REM (rapid eye movement) that occurs in dreams, and helps a person see a disturbing event in a calmer, less triggering manner.

Any kind of exercise or activity that gets you into your body, moving your body, and feeling its strength is positive. Certain forms of exercise, however, stand out. Abuse survivors and military veterans suffering from PTSD have found yoga to be extremely useful for grounding, feeling safe, and general healing. What is it about yoga that is so healing? Yoga is a powerful way of targeting specific areas of the body where trauma is held.

For Jackie:

"I went to a yoga class right down the street from the acting school where I was studying, and it was the first time I'd felt light in my body since I was eight. I'd been walking around feeling like lead my whole life, and then I came out of this yoga class, and I felt so free from that weight. I became obsessed. I went to yoga twice a day for two years. That was very integral to my healing."

Jackie and other survivors have found CORE energetics, another body-centered therapy, to be very healing in also unblocking energy that is in held in the body for a long time.

Trauma therapist and yoga instructor Lisa Danylchuk explains why yoga is so effective for healing the body:

"Yoga has this capacity to address a lot of different layers, and it addresses the body in this holistic way. It helps you to get into the body. There's the mental and philosophical, which is different from psychotherapy. It addresses the energetic side of things. I've seen people feel more whole, feel more grounded in their bodies. Yoga gives them more skills and resources for when there's a trigger, a memory or someone or something that brings up a traumatic imprint or memory. I think one of the most powerful things it does is build that sense of safety here first, and then slowly, that can expand out."

Certain forms of dance, such as belly dancing or other dances similar to the moves ancient temple dancers used in ancient India can be so effective because you have to really get into your body and move one of the most sexually charged areas: your hips. As part of a Landmark Education project where I had to help a community and challenge myself, I produced a small fundraiser with various women performers to help victims of crime, and I chose performing belly dancing because I had always been self-conscious of my dancing skills on stage and because belly dancing was so sensual. It was only when I started practicing that I realized how ashamed I felt of my hips from junior high days of boys and girls making fun of my body, but also, I felt almost a sense of frozenness, the energy in my pelvis was stuck. As I began to learn more, I began to realize that underneath the frozen tundra lay fear and anger.

While survivors come in all shapes and sizes and have a variety of individual health issues, as anyone in the general population, it is interesting to know that like certain reproductive cancers and other illnesses, sex abuse survivors have a high propensity for certain health issues and can respond well to specific kinds of nutritional supplements and diet. As Michelle Pick outlines in her book, *Are You Tired and Wired*, there are three different kinds of adrenal fatigue, and one kind is rampant among women who have been sexually abused. Pick outlines a whole protocol for adrenal fatigue sufferers/survivors. Many of the wise women leaders who have worked with women and trauma will tell you that often adrenal dysfunction is a direct result of sexual trauma. Thankfully, due to the work of Dr. Pick, renowned holistic women's psychiatrist Dr. Kelly Brogan, Dr. Christiane Northrup, and other holistic health practitioners, there are more ways to heal the body.

Now you see that envisioning your body as a temple is sometimes a matter of life and death. Every time I enter a physical space of women or even a virtual space of women, I always view each woman as a goddess whose body is a sacred temple. Substantial healing is possible only when you surround yourself with those who empathize and understand the havoc and devastation that has occurred if the sacred temple has been invaded, and can offer corresponding modalities to help return the temple back to its sacred state and even elevate it to a more magical, powerful level.

Chapter 7

GODDESS SELF LOVE

I find there is nothing more powerful in working with women than diving into the world of the goddess. Sometimes you need to step into the realm of the imaginary world of archetypes and mythology to help build yourself up. If you've spent enough time in your head disconnected from your body, as I have, it may seem counterintuitive to step further into the realm of fantasy and float further away from the earth and all things grounded. Yet why not put your well-honed, let's-escape-from-the-moment-and-feeling-pain imagination and cerebral mind to good use? While you distract the one part of your psyche with mythical drama, the rest of your mind and your soul can start receiving the messages it needs to.

What is it about goddesses? They're immortal, they're powerful, they experience love, hatred, betrayal, and rape like us and they usually find ways to overcome it. Goddesses are like fairytale characters, except grown-up ones where the princess/goddess, aka Artemis, decides she doesn't wish to marry, but instead lead a life as huntress on her own. Their power and allure was clearly big to draw the attention of corporations. You know something is intoxicating and appealing if companies are profiting from it. The popularity of all that is goddess flourished in the late nineties to early 2000s to the point where marketers picked up on the craze, incorporating goddess names into their marketing with Gillette's Venus razor blade for women and the explosion of Amazon (named after a race of warrior women), etc. Goddesses also offer a spicier, more accessible way to learn more about psychology, love, and relationships, as well as yourself. This is why I found psychiatrist Jean Bolen's *The Goddess in Everywoman* so powerful, because while she does not ask you to truly believe in goddesses, she asks you to see if you identify with one or several of the goddess archetypes such as Artemis, the huntress and protector of animals and supporter of sisterly relationships; Aphrodite, goddess of love and creativity; or Persephone, the goddess of the underground and of spring time.

Photographer Lisa Levart explains the inspiration behind her book *Goddess on Earth,* written after she started attending women's circles and goddess groups and realized there was a whole world that she never knew about:

"I suddenly felt robbed. I felt like someone had taken something from me and I'd never known it. I hadn't even known that it was taken. This identity of ourselves as bigger than who we are, we didn't have to look at. I felt cheated."

For Lisa, starting to learn about the goddesses was like archeology. *Goddess on Earth* captures photos of 70 women in different stages of life—maiden, mother, and crone—portraying the goddesses with whom they most identify.

"If you don't have something other than yourself to identify with, how do you get out of your little world? If you don't have a role model, if you can't see, how do you know how to be it? Goddess can be like that role model. It's honoring woman of all shapes, size, age, everything from [a] celebrity down to anybody. Any woman walking down the street is a goddess to me, and what is means is to be seen. And so many women feel unsafe. It's not just going and making a pretty picture. It's about, 'What do you have inside your soul that you want to be seen?' Many of the photo sessions have ended in crying for the women who say, 'Okay here's my soul and thank you for looking at me which such loving eyes.'"

Most of us women and especially those who have experienced trauma have internalized our pain and developed uber-inner critics. We are really good at beating ourselves. We use a variety of ways, some very unique to our own inner upbringing and experiences, and sometimes this pain we inflict upon ourselves is so destructive it is as if we are taking a whip to our psyches and therefore our souls and beating ourselves into submission. Your inner critic really needs a break. She's tired and needs a pedicure or a good bath or a chance to relax.

What if you were pretending you were an actual goddess? Replacing the whip with a fluffy pink fan? What if you started to immerse yourself into the world of goddesses from Jean Bolen's book and others so your darker side can channel the darkness into fun fantasy? Or maybe your inner critic is too damn tired to read, and just wants to come out and play? Maybe she just needs a pink fluffy fan to tickle her feet and cool herself off when she's feeling unloved. Maybe the little girl inside of her needs to be told: it's okay to come out and play, it's safe, we're going to play a game of "let's play goddesses." So, what if you started acting as if you *were* an actual *goddess*? As part of her School of Womanly Arts Training, Regena Thomashauer gave each enrollee a number of accoutrements, including a pink fluffy fan. She asked us to call fellow participants *sister goddess*. Many times we joked when calling ourselves that, but you know what? Even though we joked, I'd venture to say that I wasn't the only who thought being called that name and using that name felt *good*. It felt light. It felt sexy yet empowering. It felt really good.

Self-Love

Thinking of yourself as a Goddess is a fun yet efficient fast track to self-love. If your inner critic starts chiming in with, "You're not really a goddess, goddesses don't exist," remind her you're just playing and that you have to practice your playful powers of imagination skills to be a good mama to your kids. Right?

Goddesses are female deities to be worshipped. Is self-love even in a goddess's vocabulary? It doesn't need to be, because it is embedded or intertwined in the very essence of what it means to be a goddess. Goddesses don't hesitate to take a little nap if they're tired. They don't look at themselves in the mirror and start scouring their faces and bodies looking for tiny imperfections. They don't beat themselves up. They are brimming, even overflowing with self-love. They have so much they can share it.

Practicing self-love and goddess role-playing might lead you to wonder if it will start going to your head. Wherever this concern is coming from, whether it is from your inner critic or your cultural upbringing as a female telling you not to be too full of yourself, not to outshine others with your pride, tell this inner voice to go for a walk—a *long* walk. If you've experienced trauma, your reservoir of self-love is probably low enough that you have many, many years before the worry of turning into a conceited, vainglorious bitch becomes an issue. Of course, don't forget that the proud mama of the dog litter is called the bitch, so explore what it feels like to own that title by saying to yourself, "Yup, I'm the *bitch* of the family and I'm pretty damn hot!"

Marin Bach Antonson:

"The greatest healing that we can do is to remember our divinity, to remember the goddess inside, to heal all our human woundedness."

One way to foster self-love is to join a group of women or sister goddess mamas among whom bragging is not just encouraged, it's expected. One key component of the training in the networking groups that sprang from the former Woodhull Institute for Ethical Leadership in Women, founded by Naomi Wolf, is teaching women how to openly talk about their accomplishments and strengths and to commend their female peers for doing so. They encourage speaking about one another by sharing their female colleagues' assets and skills with another person. In other words, networking. The ideology behind Woodhull and other women's leadership groups is for women to achieve full equality in the workplace and elsewhere where they have to learn the same skills their male counterparts learn from an earlier age. For example: how to negotiate a salary, why competition can be a good thing, how to public speak, etc. Forcing yourself to talk about your strengths is a great way to start liking yourself. In Mama Gena's weekly classes, we had to come with a brag each week. Anything from, *I took a luscious bath* or *I bought myself some expensive lingerie* to *I got a new job*, and then everyone would applaud. It was such a good way to boost each other up. That kind of stuff starts to seep in!

Woodhull and other women's networking groups come from the leadership angle, Mama Gena comes from the goddess training angle, but both come from the idea of coming together as women to support each other in loving ourselves.

Most of the time, conjuring up the image of the goddess is what motivates me. The goddess is fun, sexy, and loves herself. But at times when deeper self-care is needed, I think of the Queen—not necessarily Queen Elizabeth II, but a regal female leader from any land or time period fictional or real that lights me up. It's the word and associations with it that help me tap into a different mindset. In her *The Queen's Code for Life* course and in her PAX training, Alison Armstrong describes the three different archetypes women usually incarnate in some form, depending on their life stages and situation: Temptress, Mother, and Queen. The Temptress is the sexy, playful, inviting archetype. As Armstrong points out, as women we get a lot of informal training and hear a lot in popular culture about being the Mother. And as the billion dollar make-up, beauty and fashion industry, from Hollywood to reality TV will attest, we are inundated with the how tos, the shoulds, and the should nots about the sexy, inviting, playful Temptress. If she falls from grace, we hear every sordid detail as well.

However, there's not a lot of conversation or training about the Queen. The Queen is all about self-care and prioritizing her own needs so that she can better lead and love the others in her life. She schedules time for herself. The spontaneous Temptress might scoff at the entire notion of scheduling, and the Mother focuses primarily on the scheduling of her children, even if she knows that today's moms must take some time out for themselves to raise happy, successful kids. Often, we get a lot encouragement to take care of our beauty needs, e.g., manicures, salon visits, etc. The Temptress is usually the driving force behind this. We see examples of how to be the Mother everywhere—even if it's unrealistic. But we only find slivers of the Queen here and there. We would probably find more examples of obtainable Mother role models if we valued the Queen more.

When I am co-leading women's circles, I make sure my circle sisters and I continually remind each other about self-care. Self-care is a *sine quo non* for the Queen. For her, boundaries are clearly drawn. She knows when to say no to certain obligations, whether it's volunteering at another school fundraiser or going to bed earlier so she can get rest. This is pretty effortless for the Queen, but for those of us bottle-fed on princess lore and struggling to love ourselves, it can be very difficult. How can you take care of yourself if you're still working on loving yourself?

Armstrong recommends taking a serious look at your various "realms" and taking stock of the important people in your life, what you value and, most importantly, what it is that you need to "fill your tank." This could be anything from eating a nourishing diet to getting enough rest to painting with water colors for 20 minutes every Friday and doing 10 minutes of yoga poses, even if it means getting up earlier so you can feel replenished and be ready to regally rule your life.

An example of a mama embodying the Queen and teaching others how to do so is Sara Blanchard, coach and author of *Flex Mom.* According to Sara, the most mundane yet necessary tasks like grocery shopping and scheduling dentist and doctor's appointments for our kids can stress us out and rule our lives if we don't prioritize ourselves first. It's almost as if you have to envision yourself as a modern-day benevolent queen— without the servants—when whipping out the daily calendar or iPhone and when answering a request to volunteer on the school fundraising committee. To this day, as per Sara's advice, I will ask myself when mapping out my week, "Is scheduling this errand during the girls' school day the best use of my time, or can I do this with my kids so I will have more time to get my own work project done or to do some other action of self-care (e.g., exercise, take a nap, meditate, etc.)?"

Self-Forgiveness

> *Resentment is like drinking a poison and then hoping it will kill your enemies.*
> **—Nelson Mandela**

I recently attended a workshop on how to heal from trauma, and one of the participants who had been abused by different members of her family made a powerful point about how we in society talk about forgiveness and the importance of survivors forgiving. "Forgiveness is a choice. I don't have to forgive." Her comment raises the issue of whether or not a survivor needs to forgive. I do think Mandela and others' arguments of the toxicity of *not* forgiving is powerful. As women, we are trained to always think about others' needs, so we female survivors put undue pressure upon ourselves to think we need to forgive our perpetrators. Perhaps forgiveness is indeed in our best interest, but the kind of forgiveness that I think we need to focus on with every drop of goddess queenly mama juice we have left in us, is forgiving ourselves. Forgiving oneself is another level of self-love. It pains me to even write this, but if your daughter had been raped, wouldn't you be pleading with her and hugging her with all the love you feel for her bursting inside of you and asking her to forgive herself? Harness this infinite well of love, and imagine hugging that part of you—the girl who was hurt—

and reminding her how much she is loved. Ask that girl what she needs. Chances are she just needs to be acknowledged and listened to—this deceptively simple act is an act of profound self-love.

The first time I realized how deeply I drank the poison of self-resentment was when I fled to Esalen after I had experienced a terrible break-up. I had just done a year of therapy, which had enabled me to survive that break-up, and so had started exploring different kinds of therapies. As I mentioned, I scheduled a Gestalt session inside a yurt, which, like a Red Tent, provided a pretty comforting space. It was there, when the therapist asked me to go back and imagine myself as a 15-year-old girl, that I realized that I blamed my 15-year-old self, that I considered myself irresponsible for getting so drunk I passed out, for letting myself be raped. The therapist then helped me realize how little compassion I had for the girl I once was.

I had a tiny insight into my total lack of compassion. It was only years later, at that women's festival, that my self-compassion took on a whole new level. As part of the festival, to get a small discount and also to meet other women I agreed to volunteer doing a "work share" helping run the communications desk. There I met Patti, a petite, mild-mannered yet cheerful therapist, and Maria, a woman who worked as therapist/counselor to young, primarily Hispanic women. They both worked with abuse and rape victims in different capacities, and they began telling stories about the women they worked with. Before I knew it, I was telling my story of trauma, and Patti uttered a phrase I'll never forget. It hit me like a ton of bricks: "You know you had the right to lie there naked." While I will never know the awful details of that night at age 15 since I had blacked out completely, what Patti said was so simple, yet illuminating: I, like every woman, every girl, every boy, have the right to lie there naked, to go to sleep naked and be left alone. Her phrase still stirs anger within me at the fact that what should be a basic human right—the right for a woman to be safe, yes, even if she's plastered and passed out drunk and naked—is not considered a right. Her comment also made me realize that I needed to send extra love to my adult and my teenage self.

Creating Your Own Altar

In every women's circle I lead, I find that creating a centerpiece altar is crucial. Creating your own personal altar is also essential. Perhaps you have heard meditation and alternative healers recommend building an altar. Does this seem like a nice idea, yet somehow you never get around to it? Here's another way to look at it: if a sacred church were pillaged and desecrated by a raging group of bandits or violent lunatic fundamentalists from an opposing religion, what would the most devout group of followers and the leader of the church do once the bandits had left and it was safe to go back to the church? Most likely, they would return to the church, even if it lay in rubble, and pick up the pieces. For however long it took, they would sweep, dust, and repaint that church, and then they would lay down flowers and relight candles and grieve the destruction that befell it before decorating it and making it even better than before.

If you have experienced abuse, you may feel like you are damaged goods. There is no question you have been violated.

But there is also no question that your soul, your beauty, your sacred goddess self is there, and you just need to build yourself an altar. Even a candle, a small object that has meaning to you, a rock, a leaf, a feather, your favorite gem stone, or a picture or photograph of you or someone you love or even someone you don't know but who inspires you, or a picture of a rainbow or a beautiful beach surrounded by a lush forest, whatever it is, create an altar for yourself. You could create this altar in a passageway of your home so that every time you pass by it, you can touch your heart and say a mantra or a phrase that empowers you—or just pass by and smile. Or you could create an altar by your reading area or the place where you meditate or go to sleep. In fact, you could create several altars and see how creating physical manifestations of your own devotion to yourself and your life can start to deepen your self-love.

While Britney doesn't find inspiration from goddesses, altars have played a part in her self-love. Britney began creating altars when she started therapy over 20 years ago:

"I do find it helpful to have small altars throughout my house. My first altars were where I would sit and meditate back in the early days. Now I walk for my meditations and have several altars scattered through my house. I have a shelf of women's power statutes, an area where I have photos of people who have died in my life, a shelf of tidbits from my daughter's childhood. I love walking by these areas—they keep my memories alive."

Perhaps the ultimate archetype is that of Maleficent. I will be forever grateful for experiencing Kristy Arbon's ingenuity in showing how we can develop mindful self-compassion by learning about the modern-day tale of Maleficent, the evil fairy in the *Sleeping Beauty* fairytale as told in the Angelina Jolie film. In the Maleficent archetype, we learn that she was an innocent child just as we all once were. In her story, her wings were ripped from her, a metaphor for a loss of innocence and also a common metaphor for rape, the shattering end of innocence that can haunt us until we face it and learn to heal it. For survivors, this story is particularly powerful because even if it is a fairytale, like all archetypes it comes from a shared experience. For Maleficent, as with all of us, there was a defining moment in her story, a loss of innocence and loss of naiveté. She hardens and tests her boundaries and power but then through looking after Sleeping Beauty her maternal and feminine side comes out. Kristy Arbon:

"She sees that innocence in this other young girl and she develops this fierce protection for this young girl. So, she mobilizes this power she has, this hardness, to protect this young girl. Towards the end, there's this mobilizing to an even greater degree of her power and her strength, to extend her desire for protection to the whole land that she's taking care of, so this maternal instinct that she has for this girl extends to the whole land. It's like a social activist sort of piece she has there. The personal becomes political for her. There's a forgiveness piece in there so she learns to

rise above old hurts to a forgiveness piece. Then right at the
end she gets her wings back."

These stories remind us we are not alone because, as Kristy Arbon points out, many of these stories are hundreds of years old, allowing us to feel a kinship with women—sisterhood—throughout time. By feeling less alone, we feel more connected—an integral part of our healing.

Chapter 8

UNLEASHING THE TIGRESS!

Whether you are really into attachment parenting or prefer a "free-range parenting" approach, if you are reading this book there is no question that a mama tiger is inside of you. If you doubt her existence, just conjure up the worst possible image of someone trying to harm your child and you will undoubtedly feel the ferocity of a wild beast ready to pounce on the attacker and tear him apart. The fact that she is there is a good thing, not just because it drives you onward to do everything you can to protect and nurture your daughter, but also because it's proof that you have a life force energy inside you that you can tap into in order to thrive in your life.

Don't forget the mama tiger can also be called the *tigress*. As you start to honor your mind and body and embrace sisterhood and your goddess self, you can also look deeper inside to that primal part of yourself, the tigress part that is sexual and sensual and wildly passionate.

For us survivors, our inner tigress was suppressed, and many of us turned this wild anger and passion inward into depression, self-loathing, and/or destructive behavior. Some of us didn't realize what we were capable of until we became mothers and felt an abundance of love and an almost frightening level of protectiveness toward our child. When we do start to heal and release emotions of all kinds, the genie is out of the bottle. It can be a little unnerving because we start to see how much emotion we are capable of.

Tapping into our animal side and releasing our anger is a primordial part of our healing. Jackie:

> *"When you talk about loving kindness, I bristle because I think there's been a piece of this healing journey for me that's so important in connecting to my rage and as a woman growing up in my culture as a girl you're trained to be loving and kind and nice, and it makes me fucking crazy. I'm so passionate about spreading the gift of rage. I think rage is the thing that saved me the most."*

Learning to express our anger can take time, but with guidance and patience you will feel a sense of freedom and levity. With this newfound freedom and opening, you are giving yourself the space to open to the world of sensuality and pleasure.

In almost every circle I lead, I think it is important to incorporate an element of sensuality. And I feel it is important to have a circle devoted at least partly to tapping into our sexuality on a regular basis. This is so important because women from a variety of backgrounds with a wide range of experiences who have never experienced rape or abuse also have difficulty knowing how to fully tap into their pleasure. Despite all of the advances in the women's movement, a woman's right to fully express her sexuality is distorted. It was at Mama Gena's School of Womanly Arts where I first heard the term *tigress*, the women enrolled in Mama Gena's full year program were all tigresses. These tigresses had evolved, but most women don't even know it's their right to evolve. Regena Thomashauer:

> *"[O]ur sensual evolution has lagged sadly behind. Basically, our culture still gives women only two options: you can be a virgin, or a slut. And actually, the slut inside every woman is the real virgin. That virgin is what gets the most air-time. We parade around all day in our buttoned-up corporate suits, or in sexless PTA meetings followed by Mommy and Me classes, carefully maintaining a lack of sensual aliveness in our daily lives. Take a ride on the subway, or peek inside a factory, if you want to see what I mean. And when that sensual side of a woman is buried, her life force dies.*

It helps to know our bodies are wired to receive pleasure on the largest organ in our body: our skin. The very fact that we have 34 more nerve fibers per square centimeter on our skin to men's 17 on average and the fact that have we twice as many nerve endings—8,000 on the clitoris compared to men's 4,000 on the penis—is testimony that we have what it takes to be on fire. We just need to learn to tap into it and remember that we have the right to fully own our sexuality and our pleasure.

And this is where the fun begins as you experiment with what gives you pleasure sexually and sensually. This is why masturbation is so key. You have to really get to know what Mama Gena and others freely call your *pussy,* but you can call it anything you want: yoni, golden lotus, vulva, etc. Knowing how we like to be touched is key, but increasing pleasure in general in our lives is also what gets the blood flowing in our pussies, in our minds, and all over. As numerous sex experts have pointed out, there are ways to increase and extend the female orgasm through various breathing techniques, different forms of touching, and sex toys. Today there are websites and stores selling all kinds of vibrators, lubricants, and other accessories in a safe, fun, female-friendly way. Owning a vibrator can be completely liberating, however, it isn't enough if you aren't taking care of yourself and finding ways in your daily life to turn yourself on in every sense of the term. Whatever it is that lights you up mentally, physically, spiritually, or all of the above, find time to do it *every* day.

Doing all this may seem selfish or frivolous, or maybe it seems fun but your initial reaction is, "Sounds great, but who the hell has the time, the money or the *energy* to do this?" The irony is that the more you give to yourself, the more fulfilled you will be, and your daughters will take notice. You want to be a role model for your daughters. Clearly what happens in your sex life is between you and your partner but just by taking care of your own pleasure and sexuality you can show your daughter what it is *to behave like* a sexually fulfilled happy mama. No pressure! Pussy doesn't like pressure. Be patient with yourself and keep an open mind as you explore your own path to sexual and sensual bliss.

Sexual fantasies can greatly enhance your sex life, but sometimes we can have fantasies that seem too dark. Both men and women have rape fantasies, and that is just the tip of the iceberg. There are as many different kinds of fantasies as there are people. The essential thing to know, especially for rape survivors, is that having dark fantasies is okay. You can delve into that darkness and create a tapestry of rich scenarios and images to turn yourself on. There is no shame in having a fantasy. Let your fantasies run wild.

It may seem counterintuitive that really diving into your deepest, darkest sexuality can make you a better mama, but take it from a pro, we mamas need to do this for our children.

Amy Jo Goddard:

"I think the greatest compliment that I ever hear from women is when they'll say to me, 'Doing this work has made me a better mother to my children.' I've heard that a lot. They transmit their healing. They transmit their empowerment to their daughters and their sons and they know that. The work has such a ripple effect. When we do

work on ourselves and we do really authentic, deep, rich work on ourselves, it can't help but help everybody in our circles. There's no way it wouldn't, so that's just so beautiful when women choose to do that healing early enough that they can hopefully course correct with their daughters and not project their experiences onto their daughters or not hinder their daughters in a way that they might have been hindered because it's just how they learned."

You have the power to rewrite your story and to recreate your fantasies. And we have full license to retell common mythologies and resurrect older buried tales. In some earlier versions of *Red Riding Hood*, there was no hunter to save Red. The original Red Riding Hood was a hell of a lot smarter and wiser than the wolf's guises. Over the centuries, the elderly woman or the crone, once depicted in Celtic and other cultures as the powerful, magical goddess, as elsewhere in history, became distorted as patriarchy turned her into a bitter, old woman. While it can be maddening to see how strong female figures have been suppressed over time, it is also empowering to know that these stories of strong heroines exist and that we can create more of them.

As Jamie Waggoner demonstrates, there is power in retelling other mythologies as a way of seeing ourselves and other women as heroines of our own lives. Jamie:

"As a storyteller, I really think that stories are kind of like DNA. There are certain key aspects to them that remain the same, but over time they will slightly morph. They

evolve as they come down through the centuries through telling and listening. With these Goddess stories, through visualization and meditation of these energies, they'll often tell me some facet or some aspect that I would not have thought of in the past."

Jamie leads workshops where she retells the classic story of the Greek goddess Persephone and has the participants act out parts of the story. In the classic tale, Persephone was lured into the underworld by Hades and raped, then condemned to spend the fall and winter in the underworld, but able to remerge in the spring and summer to be with her mother Demeter. The wilting and dying of the leaves and flowers signal Demeter's mourning the loss of her daughter to the underworld. Just thinking of this image as a mother is heartbreaking.

As Jamie retells it, Persephone was not raped by Hades, she *chose* to be with Hades. She was attracted to Hades and found her own power in the mysteries, the seductive darkness, and depths of the underworld where she became his queen. When I attended Jamie's workshop, at first a part of me, the angry hurt side, thought, "What's the point in retelling the story? Aren't we just deluding ourselves as women pretending that rape doesn't exist?" When I asked Jamie what the purpose was in retelling the story, she explained that there are many aspects to Persephone that our culture often doesn't focus on. We often don't talk about the Queen part of Persephone:

"I believe Persephone has agency. When I tell the story, I give her agency because I think that's an important thing

our women and girls need to hear. Even if someone's making
a bad choice, they're still making the choice. In my version
she has choice. She chooses to go down there. I think she is
a very, very powerful archetype for women and girls. Some
of the power lies in the fact that she does so in defiance of
expectations, her mother has a certain expectation for her
to stay at her side. We talk about boundaries, but another
caveat to that conversation is personal agency. She had a
larger purpose and was really stepping into a modality of
sovereignty and was looking for a new mentor to teach her
how to be that sovereign woman."

As Jamie explains, many people do not know that
Persephone's lover-turned-husband Hades, god of the
underworld, exercised influence over desire unnamed. When
we imagine Persephone choosing to delve into the underworld,
we can imagine ourselves rightfully claiming to engage in our
sexual fantasies and our sexual desire. We can rewrite our own
stories and fully develop our desire in all of its many forms and
permutations.

We are not denying rape exists. In fact, we are choosing
to change the culture by depicting more women who are in
charge of their sexuality and their lives. They are not victims.
They are victors.

Chapter 9

OBSTACLES

Working with women has shown me that the healing path can often be a rocky one. However, it is my hope that after reading these steps, you find that while you once equated raising your daughter through adolescence unscathed to a death-defying, daunting climb up Mount Everest, now you envision it more like a slow, steady climb of a majestic, but safer mountain. As far as your own healing is concerned, you may have once thought all the healing you could do was done, or worse, you thought that you could heal the cracks in the porcelain only so far. You now see that you can regenerate and renew your mind, body, and soul.

But old habits die hard, sister. As all the research shows, those habits of mind whether they are tired, old phrases you say to yourself or old habits of not fully taking care of yourself, those thoughts and feelings have taken years to carve neuropathways into your brain. Some experts say it takes anywhere from 45-66 days to develop new habits. When you have a number of different habits, it can be daunting to take it all on at once.

One of the greatest obstacles is doubt. As a survivor, you may have internalized your pain to the extent that you doubt your value as a person. You are so comfortable with doubt that life will feel funny without this security blanket to carry around with you to protect you from fully opening up. You have lived years doubting yourself and doubting that you can achieve full happiness. Have faith in yourself by looking at all of your sisters who have overcome tremendous excruciating pain. You *can* do this.

I have found that working with women in circle is one of the most powerful ways to heal. However, if you feel more comfortable you can enlist the help of a friend who is also on the path to self-healing. Develop a system where you hold each other accountable for self-care on all fronts. At the beginning of your journey, map out your goals, either visually through drawing a mind map (a diagram using images and words to brainstorm) and/or writing down what you wish to manifest in your life and what you wish to manifest for your daughter.

While it can take time to find women with whom you truly connect, finding sisterhood is possible. I have found in my work that there is power in finding real in *person* sisters, but online sisterhood can be very healing as well.

As Clarissa Pinkola Estés outlines in *Women Who Run With The Wolves,* despite all our best parenting efforts there will be obstacles in your path:

> *"You might well wonder if all this could be avoided. As in the animal world, a young girl learns to see the predator via her mother's and father's teachings. Without parents' loving guidance she will certainly be prey early on.... However, even with wise mothering and fathering, the young female may, especially beginning about age 12, be seduced away from her own truth by peer groups, cultural forces, or psychic pressures, and so begins a rather reckless risk-taking in order to find out for herself. When I work with older teenage girls who are convinced that the world is good if they only work it right, it always makes me feel like an old, gray-haired dog. I want to put my paws over my eyes and groan, for I see what they do not see, and I know, especially if they're willful and feisty, that they're going to insist on becoming involved with the predator at least once before they are shocked awake."*

There are no simple answers to what Dr. Estes describes. This is where I would encourage you to seek out or create a small mothering or parenting group to brainstorm ways to support your daughter, using books and other reading material for discussion and support can help supplement your learning. In your learning, you may feel like an awkward, insecure, teenager desperate to find the answers and expecting instant quick-fix solutions. Be patient and find your tribe. You will feel less alone and your growth will be faster.

Obstacles also take the form of triggers. When your daughter reaches the age at which you were raped or abused, this may be especially challenging. You will need to practice extra self-love and mindfulness during this time. This is where the role of a therapist and/or a coach can be very helpful and a solid support network of people to lean on when you are feeling vulnerable.

But little triggers can also stop you in your path. Many survivors talk about how just witnessing their daughter's pure innocence is disturbing because it reminds them of their own precious innocence before it was taken away from them. Turn these triggers around as positive reminders that the innocent girl remains within you. Your daughter is reflecting your own beauty and inner light. I find that by working in a group and together doing a ritual of honoring your own inner girl with a photograph or another symbol representing her is often very powerful.

Just following the daily news can set off what I call the re-victimization spiral. Reading or watching about a rape or child molestation story can be re-traumatizing. Obviously, you cannot shelter yourself from all news, but you can control when and how much news you take in. For peace of mind, it is best not to read or watch the news right before going to bed. If you see a headline, ask yourself if it is really necessary to read this. You can send a prayer to the victim and her family. You can send healing light or Reiki-like energy their way. Then place your hand on your heart and send yourself healing energy and say a prayer or mantra for yourself. You can also reassure yourself that thanks to the power of progressive social media such as MomsRising.org and a scores of others you can do your part to help and stay connected.

These are just some of the many obstacles, big and small, that we may face as we continue to grow. If you need more guidance on how to handle the different roadblocks along the way, please email me at: thewayofthewarriormama@gmail.com.

CONCLUSION

My fridge is still cluttered, but now a new goddess magnet has replaced Aphrodite: Durga, the Hindu goddess/ protective mother also known as Ma, the mother who promises to aid her devotees in their struggles with all of the troubles in the world if only they have the bravery to stand up and face them. At the 2017 Where Womyn Gather conference, which honors the different stages of a woman's life, this year was the year of the mother. As part of a celebratory sacred ritual, Jamie Waggoner and Ana Pilar led a Durga ritual. As Jamie explains, Durga is a multi-faceted mother and warrior goddess:

"A mom isn't just someone who nurtures. A mom is also someone who fights. Who fights battles and wins them

> *on many different levels. She seems very relevant in our society, our culture, and in a time when we're combating so many things with our current political administration, backtracking of civil rights and things that are not only insulting, but they're scary and frightening. We need a powerful woman who can compete with powerful men and come out swinging and not stop until she wins. We need someone to stand with, and to call upon, who can help us with the big battles."*

As Jamie Waggoner and the other wise women who shared their hearts, minds and spirit with me find, when we envision Durga to fight battles and when we envision protecting our daughters, we can find answers by following the Priestess way of working on three levels. First, we must work on ourselves, the foundation. You become your best, most sovereign self. Then you can help your daughter, your family, and your community fight the battles and reach their potential. Finally, you can help the world and spirit. Durga can give us the courage, the faith, and the energy to do this.

As you have seen, healing yourself and protecting your daughter are not mutually exclusive pursuits; they can work in tandem fueling each other. As you give to yourself and fill your own well, you will have more to give to your daughters and to others. By showing you ways to protect your daughter, befriend your mind, honor your body, love yourself like a goddess, embrace sisterhood and unleash the tigress within you, you have been given the keys to the kingdom of ever expansive growth and love. Like a phoenix rising from the ashes, you have done more than survive your pain. You have transmuted it and renewed your soul.

By transforming your life, you are able to carry on like a mama warrior goddess. In your strength and clarity, you will thrive while raising your daughter. It is my wish that you will find the courage and love to voice your own trauma or speak up for others' trauma. We need to break the silence and break the cycle of sexual violence. The more we speak out, the more noise we make, the more we cannot be ignored. When we voice our suffering, we break the shackles of shame. We also need to rally men and boys to the cause. A YouTube video shows the right way a guy should handle a drunk woman: wrap her in a blanket like a burrito and tuck her into bed and say good night. This is just a tiny example of how we can find ways to create a safer space for our daughters and sons. There are so many positive ways we can change our world. We owe it to mothers and daughters everywhere. I urge you to reach out, find your tribe, and never give up. We, your sisters past and present, are here for you.

REFERENCES AND RESOURCES

For a more extensive list of resources and references, please go to
www.thewayofthewarriormama.com.

Meg Tobin, therapist, trauma resiliency expert
www.breathingspacestudio.com

Alison J. Stone, LCSW
Gestalt therapist
212-560-5690

Jamie Waggoner writer, storyteller, teacher
www.jamiewaggoner.com
www.helloshakti.com

Amy Jo Goddard, sexual empowerment expert, speaker, and author of Woman on Fire
    info@amyjogoddard.com
    AmyJoGoddard.com

Kristy Arbon, self-compassion and mindfulness teacher
    kristyarbon.com

Gina Martin, licensed acupuncturist
    www.triplespiralhealingarts.com

Susan Ford Collins, author of *Our Children Are Watching*, part of *The Technology of Success* series
    www.technologyofsuccess.com

Marin Bach-Antonson, healer, coach, and creator of the Priestess Rising Program
    www.riseupgoddess.com

Alisa Starkweather
    http://new.alisastarkweather.com
    Red Tent Temple Movement
    http://redtenttemplemovement.com

Princess Warriors
    Rhonda Fleischer, Founder
    www.princesswarriors.org

Cea Sunrise Person, author of *North of Normal: A Memoir of My Wilderness Childhood, My Unusual Family, and How I Survived Both*
    ceaperson.com

Lisa Danylchuk, trauma therapist, yoga instructor, and author *How You Can Heal,*
    howwecanheal.com

Lisa Levart, photographer and author of *Goddess on Earth*
    goddessonearth.com
    www.lushphotography.com

Alison Armstrong, educator and expert on understanding men, Cofounder of PAX Programs
    Understanding Men workshops (formerly The Queen's Code workshop)
    understandmen.com/programs/for_women/

Sara Blanchard, author and coach
    www.flexmombook.com

Linda Graham, psychotherapist and author of *Bouncing Back: Rewiring Your Brain For Maximum Resilience and Well Being.*
    lindagraham-mft.net

Elizabeth Nahum, healer and founder of the New Avalon Centre for Women's Mysteries www.elizabethnahum.com/Elizabeth_Nahum/Home.html

Red Tent Temple Movement
    redtenttemplemovement.com/about/

Online Red Tent Group
    www.facebook.com/groups/762092977165359/

Where Womyn Gather, Women's Spirituality Festival
    www.wherewomyngather.com

Mama Gena's School of Womanly Arts
www.mamagenas.com

News Stories
Abduction, Often Violent, a Kyrgyz Wedding Rite, by Craig S. Smith, April 30, 2005
www.nytimes.com/2005/04/30/world/asia/abduction-often-violent-a-kyrgyz-wedding-rite.html

Grab and Run: Kyrgyzstan's Bride Kidnappings, by Noriko Kayashi / Panos, November 4, 2013
www.newsweek.com/grab-and-run-1634

Films
Finding Kind, documentary and campaign
www.kindcampaign.com/documentary/

13 Reasons Why
www.netflix.com/title/80117470

Sexual education, Sexual Assault Advocacy, etc.

Rape, Abuse and Incest National Network, the nation's largest anti-sexual violence organization
www.rainn.org
Get Help 24/7 1800-656-HOPE (4673)

National Online Resource Center on Violence Against Women:
vawnet.org

Books
American Girls: Social Media and the Secret Lives of Teenagers, by Nancy Jo Sales

Are You Tired and Wired?, by Michelle Pick

Women Who Run with the Wolves, by Clarissa Pinkola Estés

The Talk: What Your Kids Need to Hear from You About Sex, by Sharon Maxwell Ph.D.
   www.drsharonmaxwell.com

Goddesses in Everywoman, by Jean Shinoda Bolen

Girls & Sex: Navigating the Complicated New Landscape, by Peggy Orenstein

Misconceptions, by Naomi Wolf

Promiscuities: The Secret Struggle for Womanhood, by Naomi Wolf

Simplicity Parenting: Using the Extraordinary Power of Less to Raise Calmer, Happier, and More Secure Kids, Kim John Payne and Lisa M. Ross

Opening Up by Writing It Down, Third Edition: How Expressive Writing Improves Health and Eases Emotional Pain, by James W. Pennebaker Ph.D.

Writing Down Your Soul, by Janet Connor

Breathe, Mama, Breathe: 5-Minute Mindfulness for Busy Moms, by Shonda Moralis

The Courage to Heal: A Guide for Women Survivors of Child Sexual Abuse, by Ellen Bass and Laura Davis

The Body Keeps Score: Brain, Mind and Body in the Healing of Trauma, by Bessel Van der Kolk

Women's Bodies, Women's Wisdom, by Christiane Northrup

Trauma and Recovery: The Aftermath of Violence—From Domestic Abuse to Political Terror, by Judith L. Herman

Yes Means Yes! Visions of Female Sexual Power and A World Without Rape, by Jaclyn Friedman and Jessica Valenti

Transforming a Rape Culture, Emilie Buchwald, Pamela Fletcher, and Martha Roth, Editors

The Macho Paradox: Why Some Men Hurt Women and How All Men Can Help, by Jackson Katz

The Color of Violence: The Incite! Anthology, by INCITE Women of Color Against Violence

I Never Called It Rape, by Robin Warshaw

The Red Tent, by Anita Diamant

Against Our Will: Men, Women, and Rape, by Susan Brownmiller

Myths and Facts About Male Victims of Rape, by Men Against Sexual Violence

Therapy
EMDR
    www.emdria.org/? page=emdr_therapy

Eye movement desensitization and reprocessing (EMDR) therapy in the treatment of depression: a matched pairs study in an inpatient setting

www.ncbi.nlm.nih.gov/pmc/articles/PMC4467776/

EFT, Emotional Freedom Technique or Tapping
www.emofree.com/eft-tutorial/eft-tapping-tutorial.html

Institute of Core Energetics
www.coreenergetics.org/4-year-core-energetics-practitioner-certification-program/

ACKNOWLEDGEMENTS

Many different kinds of warriors helped make this possible. Thank you to Meg Tobin for being there that night at the Red Tent and for all your support since then. Thank you to my husband for feeding my heart, soul, and grumbling tummy, and being the best daddy possible to our girls. Thank you to my daughters for reminding me every day what matters most.

Thank you to my mom and dad and my brothers and sisters for the countless ways you have loved and helped me. Thank you to all of the brave warrior goddesses I interviewed who shared their stories of pain and healing. The Author Incubator genius Angela Lauria, who gave me the courage and the guidance to push forward and tell my story. Maggie McReynolds, aka book midwife, for your editing expertise and compassionate heart.

Thank you to Rozanne Els for her thorough and insightful research.

Thank you to all of the circle mamas, Elena Schloss, Lisa Larson-Kelley, Louise Male, Rebecca Lazaroff, and Rhonda Fleischer, for your unconditional love and for bringing sisterhood and motherhood to a whole new level. Thank you to soul sister and coach Heather Gray for first helping me to realize I could write a book. Thank you to soul sister Robin Levy for being part of our writing circle years ago. Thank you to Dr. Judith Kiersky and Dr. Ellen Frost for your initial help years ago. Thank you to Marin Bach-Antonson, who first introduced me to mama circling, sisterhood, and priestessing. Thank you to my midwife Martha Roth who allowed me to claim a sacred rite of passage: giving birth to both my daughters at home. Thank you to Kristy Arbon for reminding me throughout the book-writing process to be compassionate to myself, and for all of your heart-filled wisdom. Thank you to Alisa Starkweather for your powerful advice and for our transformative conversation. Thank you to everyone who has helped me along the way.

To the Morgan James Publishing team: Special thanks to David Hancock, CEO & Founder for believing in me and my message. To my Author Relations Manager, Margo Toulouse, thanks for making the process seamless and easy. Many more thanks to everyone else, but especially Jim Howard, Bethany Marshall, and Nickcole Watkins.

ABOUT THE AUTHOR

Sally Clark is a mama, a writer, a director, and an artist.

Raised in cowgirl country in Calgary, Alberta, Canada, Sally's passion for helping women and girls reclaim their power grew from her experiences far away from the Rocky Mountains and the cowboy's cohort—in Paris, France and New York City, where she began working on documentary films that investigated the abuses of cult leaders, the effects of pollution on the environment and human sexuality, and the Ecstasy drug problem among teenagers.

After graduating from Columbia University's Graduate School of Journalism, Sally worked for Naomi Wolf on her book *Misconceptions: Truth, Lies, and the Unexpected on the Journey to Motherhood;* for Dalma Heyn on her book *Drama Kings: The Men Who Drive Strong Women Crazy;* and worked with Lili Fournier, producer of the *Women of Wisdom and Power* series about the Mount Holyoke teen girls' leadership program, *Take the Lead.* In 2000, Sally launched Cowgirl Productions and delved into the lives of the brave, savvy, and unfettered women of rodeo. A graduate of *Mama Gena's School of Womanly Arts* and of *Queen's Code* author Alison Armstrong's *Understanding Men and Women* workshops, Sally worked as a teacher and advisory board member for the nonprofit *Act Now,* which teaches film and leadership skills to preteen girls. A survivor of sexual trauma, Sally produced an artist fundraiser for the nation's largest victims' assistance organization, *Safe Horizon,* where she belly danced as part of a self-imposed dare.

In addition to coaching and co-leading women's circles, Sally does the daily dance of marriage with the light and love of her life, raises little daughter-warrior-goddesses-in-training, and finds time to stop and smell the flowers. Sally lives with her husband and two daughters in New York's Hudson Valley.

THANK YOU

Thank you for taking time out of your busy parenting life to read this book!

By choosing to learn about the way of the warrior mama you know that you are not alone in your journey to helping your daughter and to healing your life.

To receive a free class on the three secrets of warrior mamas, please email me at: thewayofthewarriormama@gmail.com.

I look forward to hearing from you.

With gratitude,
Sally

Morgan James
Speakers Group

www.TheMorganJamesSpeakersGroup.com

We connect Morgan James published
authors with live and online events
and audiences who will benefit
from their expertise.

Morgan James makes all of our titles available
through the Library for All Charity Organization.

www.LibraryForAll.org